Doug Fields

ZondervanPublishingHouse
Grand Rapids, Michigan

A Division of HarperCollins*Publishers*

Youth Specialties Books

Professional Resources

Advanced Peer Counseling in Youth Groups
Called to Care
The Church and the American Teenager *(previously released as Growing Up in America)*
Developing Spiritual Growth in Junior High Students
Developing Student Leaders
Feeding Your Forgotten Soul
Help! I'm a Volunteer Youth Worker!
High School Ministry
How to Recruit and Train Volunteer Youth Workers *(previously released as Unsung Heroes)*
Junior High Ministry (Revised Edition)
The Ministry of Nurture
Organizing Your Youth Ministry
Peer Counseling in Youth Groups
The Youth Minister's Survival Guide
Youth Ministry Nuts and Bolts
110 Tips, Time-savers, and Tricks of the Trade

Discussion Starter Resources

Amazing Tension Getters
Get 'Em Talking
High School TalkSheets
Junior High TalkSheets
More High School TalkSheets
More Junior High TalkSheets
Option Plays
Parent Ministry TalkSheets
Tension Getters
Tension Getters Two
To Do or Not To Do

Special Needs and Issues

The Complete Student Missions Handbook
Divorce Recovery for Teenagers
Ideas for Social Action

Ideas Library

Ideas Combo 1-4, 5-8, 9-12, 13-16, 17-20, 21-24, 25-28, 29-32, 33-36, 37-40, 41-44, 45-48, 49-52
Ideas Index

Youth Ministry Programming

Adventure Games
Creative Bible Lessons
Creative Programming Ideas for Junior High Ministry
Creative Socials and Special Events
Good Clean Fun
Good Clean Fun, Volume 2
Great Fundraising Ideas for Youth Groups
Great Games for City Kids
Great Ideas for Small Youth Groups
Greatest Skits on Earth
Greatest Skits on Earth, Volume 2
Holiday Ideas for Youth Groups (Revised Edition)
Hot Illustrations for Youth Talks
Hot Talks
Junior High Game Nights
More Junior High Game Nights
On-Site: 40 On-Location Youth Programs
Play It! Great Games for Groups
Play It Again! More Great Games for Groups
Road Trip
Rock Talk
Super Sketches for Youth Ministry
Teaching the Bible Creatively
Teaching the Truth About Sex
Up Close and Personal: How to Build Community in Your Youth Group
The Youth Specialties Handbook for Great Camps & Retreats

4th-6th Grade Ministry

Attention Grabbers for 4th-6th Graders
4th-6th Grade TalkSheets
Great Games for 4th-6th Graders
How to Survive Middle School
Incredible Stories
More Attention Grabbers for 4th-6th Graders
More Great Games for 4th-6th Graders
More Quick and Easy Activities for 4th-6th Graders
Quick and Easy Activities for 4th-6th Graders
Teach 'Toons

Clip Art

ArtSource™ Volume 1—Fantastic Activities
ArtSource™ Volume 2—Borders, Symbols, Holidays, and Attention Getters
ArtSource™ Volume 3—Sports
ArtSource™ Volume 4—Phrases and Verses
ArtSource™ Volume 5—Amazing Oddities and Appalling Images
ArtSource™ Volume 6—Spiritual Topics
Youth Specialties Clip Art Book
Youth Specialties Clip Art Book, Volume 2

Video

Edge TV Volumes 1-9
God Views
Next Time I Fall in Love Video Curriculum
Promo Spots for the Junior High Game Nights
Resource Seminar Video Series
Understanding Your Teenage Video Curriculum
Witnesses

Student Books

Going the Distance
Good Advice
Grow for It Journal
Grow for It through the Scriptures
How to Live with Your Parents without Losing Your Mind
I Don't Remember Dropping the Skunk, But I Do Remember Trying to Breathe
Next Time I Fall in Love
Next Time I Fall in Love Journal
101 Things to Do During a Dull Sermon

Youth Specialties

Creative Bible Lessons on the Life of Christ

Youth Specialties Books are published by Youth Specialties, 12224 Greenfield Drive, El Cajon, California 92021.

Doug Fields
Interior design and typography by PAZ Design Group
Cover designed by Rhombus Design Group

Printed in the United States of America

ISBN: 0-310-40251-4

00 01 02 03 / ML / 12 11 10 9 8

Dedication

This book is dedicated to the committed youth workers who helped me see Jesus through their teaching and lifestyle: Bill Bower, Jim and Cathy Burns, Marty Driggs, Mike Driggs, Randy Largent, Rick Larsh, Gary Lenhart, Gail McKay, Sydney Perry, Craig Sanders, Pam Sears, Brent and Dawn Watson, Doug Webster, and Gary Webster.

Special thanks

Many of the ideas in this book come from collaboration with good friends, gifted brains, and quality youth workers: Cathy Fields, Eddie James, Keith Page, Scott Rachels, Chris Schmaltz, and David Walter. Appreciation is also extended to my youth ministry students at Southern California College for trying these ideas with their youth groups and providing me valuable feedback. Also, this book wouldn't have been published if it weren't for Noel Becchetti having the idea, the editing skills, and the patience. Finally, thanks goes to Linda Kaye for her partnership in ministry and her invaluable assistance with everything involved in *Making Young Lives Count.*

About the author

Doug Fields, founder and director of *Making Young Lives Count*, is a national public speaker, college professor, and author of over a dozen books including *Help! I'm a Volunteer Youth Worker* (Youth Specialties). He also serves as youth pastor at Saddleback Church in Mission Viejo, California.

For further information regarding *Making Young Lives Count* or a brochure of more resources, please call or write Doug Fields at:

MAKING YOUNG LIVES COUNT
21612 Plano Trabuco Rd. #Q-30
Trabuco Canyon, CA 92679
Phone and Fax: (714) 459-9517

TABLE OF CONTENTS

Introduction

This book is designed to provide you with a tool that will help you to teach about Jesus in a refreshing way. If you are already a creative teacher, these ideas can act as a springboard for greater creativity. If you appreciate a little creative help, these ideas are ready to go—all you have to do is implement them.

While the methods of instruction vary, the messages are consistent. They are designed to lead your students to understand more about Jesus and move them toward a stronger commitment to their faith. Students will learn that Jesus was more than just a "good man." They will learn about Him in ways they've probably never before experienced. And the more they know about Jesus, the more they will know about God.

Look over the first three chapters before you jump into the studies. If you're a veteran, they'll be reminders; if you're new to youth ministry, they'll give you a foundation to be a more effective teacher.

I hope this book will be a helpful tool for you. More importantly, I hope this book helps your students to see Jesus in a new way, and that their lives will be different through God's grace and your commitment to teach them about the Way, the Truth, and the Life.

Blessings from a fellow youth worker.

Doug Fields
Creative Bible Lessons on the Life of Christ

WHY USE CREATIVITY IN YOUR TEACHING?

I can't recall any students in my years of youth ministry who have come running to youth group screaming, "Give me another Bible talk, Doug! I can't get enough of them." Most students manage to sit still through youth talks week after week (key word: "most") only because they know there's a lot more to youth group than just the talk.

When the talk is packaged creatively, however, students are usually much more interested in learning God's truth (key word: "usually"). Using a creative approach isn't the cure-all to energizing the apathetic or uninterested student, but it does help. Not only does creative teaching capture your students' attention, it also communicates to them that you're willing to do whatever it takes to get the message across. They see you adapting your teaching style in order to enlighten them with God's timeless truths.

There are three reasons why I get excited about creative teaching:

Creative teaching makes Sunday School and youth group exciting.

The word "boring" has been defined as doing the same thing over and over again. And it has been said that insanity is doing the same thing over and over again while expecting different results. If both of these are true, many youth groups are BORING and their leaders are INSANE. Teaching the same way over and over gets boring . . . no matter how great a communicator we may be.

Our Sunday school programs and youth groups should shatter the stereotype that church is boring. I'm not suggesting we turn our youth ministries into circuses so they're not dull, but I am suggesting we think through why we do what we do and why we teach the way we teach.

When time is invested in creativity, it makes youth group a different place. Sunday school gets exciting; youth meetings become fun. The truths within God's Word are exciting—let's make our teaching methods equally exciting.

Students learn in different ways.

I learn best by doing. My wife learns better when she listens and takes notes. My older sister learns best while reading and my younger sister learns best through observing. We are all from the same family, yet we all have different learning styles.

If we always teach the same way, we'll reach only a fraction of our students. Unfortunately, chances are high that the small group we reach will only learn "pieces" from our styles, because they probably have additional learning styles that complement their dominant styles.

If students learn in different ways, we would be wise to teach with different methods if we're going to minister effectively. I have a sign above my desk that constantly challenges the way I teach. It reads: THERE ARE SEVERAL ANGLES TO THE HEART. If I keep pounding away at one angle, I lose an opportunity to reach the entire heart.

Students actually look forward to learning.

Imagine having students who look forward to learning from God's Word. It's possible, and even probable as we develop creative teaching methods and make ourselves open to new approaches.

Thankfully, I learned this lesson in my first few years of ministry. I always wanted to be a great youth speaker and in my early years I spent a lot of time putting talks together. I thought I gave great talks. They were biblical—mixed with powerful stories, illustrations, humor, and personal application. I traded off teaching Sunday school every other week with a woman named Robin. Robin didn't give talks. She'd break the students into small groups, assign them different passages to read, and then had them develop their passages into mini-dramas. These students would then act out the passage and discuss their understanding of the Scripture. That's it! Robin didn't define any theological terms, she presented no current statistics, gave no three-point sermons, and put in little preparation time. The students loved it when Robin taught (I still have a tough time calling it teaching). When I would finish one of my "great" talks, students would quickly approach me and ask, "Is Robin going to teach next week?" They didn't say, "That was great! It changed my life." They commented more on what Robin wasn't teaching than on what I taught them. It was very depressing. I always wanted to shout, "Robin isn't even teaching . . . she's . . . uh . . . facilitating." Then it hit me: Most students enjoyed Robin's methods because they were involved and they were learning more. Because of this, they looked forward to her teaching time.

It's an awesome responsibility and privilege to teach God's Word. The message is life-changing! The methods of communicating the message are open for development and experimentation. My prayer is that you will be open for a little variation. The results will be worth your effort . . . and some students eventually will thank you for it (key words: "some" and "eventually").

TEN COMPONENTS OF EFFECTIVE TEACHING

My intention for this chapter isn't to provide you with a doctoral thesis on methods of biblical instruction. There are several outstanding books available on teaching methods. In this chapter I want to highlight ten ways students learn. I'm sure there are more, but these are the ten I keep in front of me as I prepare a lesson. I use this list as a reminder of how students learn and as a challenge for me to use a different method than I used before.

Doing

When you are able to get your students to do something with your message, you have succeeded! Participation shoots a student's learning curve straight up.

I could teach on servanthood for six years, and my students could have all the head knowledge needed to articulate a theology of service and proudly quote a few Scriptures, but it doesn't mean they'll be servants. When I provide an opportunity for my students to serve a widow in our church, they learn more about servanthood through this one act than by hours of listening to me talk.

The Christian faith can be experienced, and your students will become more mature, when you give them opportunities to experience and practice God's truth.

Seeing

Many of your students were weaned on Sesame Street and MTV and are accustomed to learning through observation. They watch loads of TV and are primed to learn through this medium. When you can make your message one they can see, you create a visual memory that will last for a significant length of time.

Acting

As I mentioned in the last chapter, many students love the opportunity to read Scripture and act out their interpretations. Acting gets your students up, moving, involved, interacting, and thinking of how God's Word might be translated in today's vernacular. This medium helps cement passages into your students' memories.

Writing

Creative writing or the expression of feelings on paper is an effective way for adolescents to communicate and learn. Many students "dabble" with poetry or songwriting; they can apply these methods to exploring biblical truths when given the opportunity.

Creating

I stumbled across this method when I asked a few students to help me put a sermon together for our adult congregation. They had great ideas, refreshing insights, and applicable illustrations. These students provided me with so much help, I asked them to come back every week and help me create youth messages and lessons. They loved the opportunity to interact with me in a new way and felt as if they were in the "inner circle." This opportunity challenged these students to own the creation of a message or lesson. They would search the Scriptures, think of creative methods to communicate its truths, and assure me of its relevance and application for their peers.

Playing

I'll never forget my fifth-grade Sunday school teacher explaining a Bible bingo game. It may seem like a stupid idea now, but at the time I couldn't believe she said the "G" (game) word at church. I didn't think we were supposed to play games at Sunday school. We had so much fun playing Bible bingo that Mrs. Miller created new Bible games every week. The joy of playing and discovery is one that I'll always remember, while some of the spiritual truths I learned in her class I will never forget.

Hearing

Few students learn best by listening to a teacher. They still may learn, but lecturing is one of the least effective forms of communication.

What increases the effectiveness of teaching through speaking is when stories are used. As you know, storytelling was a favorite method used by Jesus, and it was very effective. Though students won't admit it, I'm convinced they still love stories. Your teenagers have heard hundreds of stories during their childhood; if given a choice between listening to a talk or hearing a good story, I'm sure they'll choose the story every time.

Drawing

Some of the most creative and artistic students in your youth group are the last people who will volunteer to act out or publicly share their feelings. Many artistic students are reserved and choose to express themselves through their art. Give them an opportunity to share their faith by drawing what they "see" from Scripture. Give them a passage and allow them to interpret it through their drawing. You'll see some interesting results, and you'll minister to students who are hard to reach through traditional methods.

Cooperating

Some of your students may learn best by working with other students. I know some highly relational students who can't do anything alone, but when given the opportunity to work with others, they discover a new depth of understanding.

Living

This last component is directed to you as the teacher. Your students are learning much from you and how you live your life. They are absorbing messages about God's love and the Christian faith each time they interact with you or watch you in action. Don't underestimate the power of your lifestyle.

I really don't remember very many messages I heard as a teenager, but the truths I observed in my leaders made a lasting impression. Adolescents are quick to sniff out phonies. They are looking for real people to be real models of what it means to love God and live as a Christian. Maybe that's why James wrote in his letter, "Not many of you should presume to be teachers, my brothers, because you know that we who teach will be judged more strictly" (James 3:1).

HOW TO USE THIS BOOK

There is no one way to use this book. The ideas and methods presented can be implemented in many different ways. Your concern shouldn't be about how well you pulled off a given idea, but rather on how well your students are learning about Jesus. If they have a lot of fun but don't learn anything about Jesus, the purpose for these studies has been missed.

I know youth ministry, and I know how to communicate to the students in my youth group—but I don't know your students. No one knows your group better than you. The ideas presented throughout this book will work in general, but feel free to tweak these ideas to work for you specifically. The ideas in this book are not infallible. If one doesn't work for you, get rid of it or use it as a springboard for another idea that will work for your students.

Let me go over a few steps on how you can use these creative Bible lessons effectively.

Familiarize yourself with the lesson format

To bring some type of continuity to the twelve lessons in this book, I've chosen these five components:

Introduction. The ideas presented under this section are designed to hook the student's interest in a light, fun, and upbeat manner. Some of the ideas may be used as games; others are intended to be humorous. Most of the ideas require little preparation—some photocopying, some supplies, and a few writing materials, and you'll be ready. The main point to remember for the introductions is to utilize them informally. Try these ideas as crowd breakers; allow the students to have fun, get up from their seats, interact, and begin the lesson on a light note.

Participation. The ideas presented under this section are designed to involve the students with one of the main points of the lesson. Like the introduction, this section gets students up and moving and interacting with one another. The ideas under this section don't necessarily tie directly in to the thesis of the lesson, but are designed to set up the central point.

Observation. The ideas presented under this section are designed to let the students "see" part of the lesson. These ideas will help students make a visual connection with the lesson. In most cases, the observation will set up the instruction time and lead into the teaching. On three occasions where the observation comes after the teaching (Lessons One, Two, and Nine), the observation reinforces what's already been taught.

Instruction. The ideas presented under this section are designed to help you communicate a few biblical truths to your students. I realize you will be able to find additional interpretations of a selected passage. Use what fits best with your style, your beliefs, and your group. I don't claim to be a theologian. The presented truths are the answers I came up with when I asked myself, "Why is this in the Bible and what does it mean to students today?" These instructional ideas are intended to give you direction as distinct from being complete youth talks. If you want your students to investigate the Scripture text a bit further, use the extra questions in the feature called "Digging In." These questions will encourage your students to dig into the text for the answers.

Application. The ideas presented under this section are designed to help students immediately apply the biblical truth that was taught. In some lessons, there are action steps for students to take or items they may bring home. The goal of this section is to help answer the "so what" question, and show how the lesson relates to students' lives.

Estimate your time

Each lesson is designed to be completed in approximately fifty minutes. Since each youth group and teaching setting varies, carefully read through each lesson and make any time adjustments you feel might be necessary. You may find that you can't use all the material within the time you have. That's okay! Use what works in the amount of time you have and save the remaining material for another meeting.

Take time to prepare

This book was written to cut down your preparation time, not eliminate it altogether. Read through each lesson at least a couple hours prior to teaching it. Most of your preparation time will include reading the lesson, photocopying the handouts, and gathering a few materials. (If you have the same luck with copy machines as I do, don't wait until the last minute to copy your handouts.) These handouts will really add to the quality "feel" of each lesson.

Also, spend a few minutes thinking through the transitions from one section to the next (for example, from participation to instruction). Some of the transitions contain specific bridge comments, while others need you to provide the bridge sentence or instruction to make the flow more understandable.

Add your own creativity

Are you one of those people who claim that you don't have a creative bone in your body? Well, aside from that not being true, you can rest in the fact that the essence of creativity lies in your ability to copy these ideas and adapt them to your situation.

If you have some additional preparation time, spend it thinking through how you can take the provided ideas a step further with more personalized illustrations or applications.

Be flexible

If you experience a situation where a student or students begin to share a hurt or need some personal ministry time, be ready to adapt. If life change is happening during the participation section, don't force yourself into the instruction section. Let it go—even if you're running out of time. God may have a different agenda from yours. Being flexible allows God to work on His timing.

I've found that most of God's "divine appointments" come at times I didn't plan. The goal of educating your students is to be effective, not necessarily efficient.

Adapt to your group size

Don't get caught in the trap of saying, "This won't work with the size of my group." Think through each section and brainstorm ways you can make an idea either bigger or smaller.

Keep God in the process

Let's face it, we can fool anyone about the depth of our spirituality. Well, anyone except God. You'll find greater wisdom, strength, and patience when you commit your role as a leader, and each of these lessons, to God. God doesn't expect you to be the greatest teacher ever; He doesn't even expect you to have your own life completely together. But God does want you to do the possible and have faith that He will do the impossible.

We have this treasure in jars of clay to show that this
all-surpassing power is from God and not from us.
II Corinthians 4:7

LESSON ONE

JESUS AS GOD

JOHN 14:5-11; 20:24-29

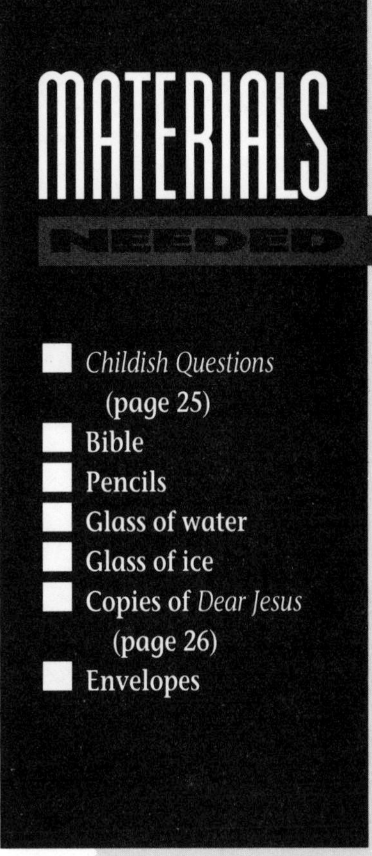

- *Childish Questions* (page 25)
- Bible
- Pencils
- Glass of water
- Glass of ice
- Copies of *Dear Jesus* (page 26)
- Envelopes

Overview

This lesson is designed to teach students that Jesus was both human and divine. Jesus was God in the flesh. This lesson also shows that many people have questioned Jesus' claim of deity, including His closest followers. It's intended to challenge students to move to a place in their faith where they can say, "Jesus, my Lord and my God."

Introduction (5 minutes)

This section gets students thinking about a few of the different and difficult questions people may have about God.

1) Find a book that has questions or quotes about God from children (such as *101 Questions Children Ask about God* by David Veerman, 1990, Tyndale House Publishers, or *Children's Letters to God* by E. Marshall and S. Hample, 1991, Workman Publishers). If you have a difficult time finding one of these books, you can use the examples from *Childish Questions* (page 25).

2) Start your lesson by reading the humorous things children say about God.

3) Give students a chance to add their own questions or things they wondered about God as children.

4) After you read a few of the statements, say, **It's normal to have questions about God. There are a lot of things about God that are difficult to understand. One of the difficulties is understanding how Jesus can be God. That's what we're talking about today.**

Participation (15-20 minutes)
This section gets your students thinking about how ridiculous it is to think a human being could be equal with God.

1) Tell the students that for the next few minutes they are to pretend they are God and have the power to do anything. In their role as God, they may change any situation or create anything they want, as long as the effect would be positive. They should come up with as many ideas as they can in ten minutes. Tell them to focus their ideas and actions in four categories:

- personal
- family
- school
- world

Encourage students to be creative and have fun, but also to tackle some of the difficult issues in their lives and in the world.

2) Have students write each of their different actions on separate sheets of paper. When they've finished, students may get up and tape their ideas to four different walls that you have marked with the appropriate categories (personal, family, school, and world).

3) After the ideas are taped on the wall, go from wall to wall and encourage the students to explain and discuss the actions they listed.

Instruction (10-15 minutes)
This section helps your students understand that Jesus did claim to be God, and even some of His closest followers struggled with that claim.

1) Now that your students have pretended to play God, ask them to identify some of the major differences between God and humans. Be prepared to draw out their answers; help them to really think about the differences.

2) After your students have shared some of the differences, ask if they agree or disagree with the following statement:

> **Since Jesus was human and claimed to be God, it's possible for one of us to also be like God.**

3) After soliciting their responses to the previous statement, explain that many people, churches, and

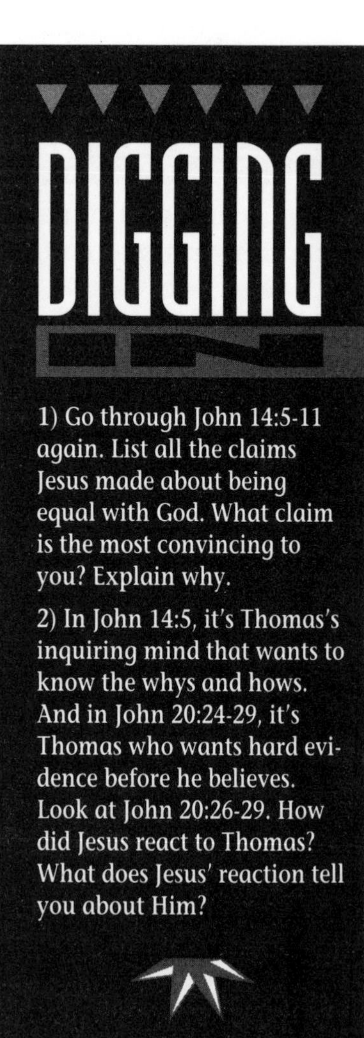

1) Go through John 14:5-11 again. List all the claims Jesus made about being equal with God. What claim is the most convincing to you? Explain why.

2) In John 14:5, it's Thomas's inquiring mind that wants to know the whys and hows. And in John 20:24-29, it's Thomas who wants hard evidence before he believes. Look at John 20:26-29. How did Jesus react to Thomas? What does Jesus' reaction tell you about Him?

religions claim to know the way to God, and the truth about God; some people even claim to be God or be like God.

4) Read aloud John 14:5-11. Emphasize that Jesus claimed to be God ("Anyone who has seen me has seen the Father," verse 9).

5) Explain that even those who were the closest to Jesus still had a difficult time believing His claim. Read John 20:24-29. Even a disciple, Thomas, had trouble believing Jesus was God.

6) Make the following two observations:

a) Thomas required evidence to believe Jesus was really God. He needed to see that Jesus had risen from the dead.

b) Thomas's doubt eventually resulted in belief. He exclaimed, "My Lord and my God!"

7) Reemphasize that Jesus wasn't only a human—He was God.

Observation (5 minutes)
This section helps your students to begin to grasp the mystery that Jesus was both fully God and fully human, and that He didn't give up His divine nature when He became a human.

1) Say, **Many people get frustrated because they can't understand how Jesus could be both human and divine, two distinctively different natures, at the same time. I want to help you try to understand this difficult truth by showing you how this is true in another area.**

2) Hold up a glass of ice and ask students what ice consists of. (Answer: frozen water or water.)

3) Hold up a glass of water and ask students what elements water consists of. (Surprise answer: water!)

4) Your students should observe that ice and water are two manifestations of the same element. Ice and water have different properties, but they come from the same source.

5) Explain that this is similar to Jesus' two natures. Both are different, yet the same. Jesus was clearly human; yet truly God as well! Say, **Even when we have doubts and questions, the fact remains: Jesus is God!**

Application (10 minutes)
This section allows your students the opportunity to express their feelings and questions about God.

1) Explain that God isn't surprised or upset by our questions. It is normal for Christians to have doubts, and a discussion like today's usually generates a lot of questions.

2) Let students know they are going to write a letter to God, expressing their faith as well as their questions, as they begin this series on the person of Jesus.

3) Pass out copies of the *Dear Jesus* letterhead (page 26) and plain white envelopes to each student.

4) Tell your students to begin writing their letters. Encourage them to be honest with God about the doubts and questions they might have. Challenge them to ask God to show them specific evidence that would help them to respond as Thomas eventually did, "My Lord and my God!"

5) When students have finished, they should seal their letter in their envelope and write their name on the envelope. Collect these letters and tell your students that they will get them back at the end of the twelve-week series.

Childish Questions

From the book *101 Questions Children Ask about God* by David Veerman.

Does God sleep, or does He just rest?

How does God make the sun and moon go up and down?

Did God make people in outer space?

If God made spiders, why do people squish them?

How can Jesus fit in my heart?

Is there a McDonalds in heaven?

Why doesn't God just zap the bad people?

Here is an example from the book *Children's Letters to God* by E. Marshall and S. Hample.

Dear God,

Church is all right, but you could sure use better music. I hope this does not hurt your feelings.

Dear Jesus,
I want to express a few things I know about You. They are . . .
I want to express how I feel about You. I feel . . .
I want to express some questions I have about You. They are . . .

LESSON TWO

JESUS AS HUMAN

MATTHEW 4:1-11

MATERIALS NEEDED

- Copy of the video *What About Bob?*
- Television
- VCR
- Deck of playing cards
- Prizes for a rigged game
- *The Seven P's of Puberty* (page 31)
- *Jesus as a teen* (page 32)
- Overhead projector *(optional)*

Introduction (10-20 minutes)
This section introduces the theme of playing by the rules.

1) Rent the video *What About Bob?*, starring Bill Murray and Richard Dreyfuss.*

2) Introduce the clip by saying, **This clip features Bob, who lies to see his vactioning counselor. Watch how Bob breaks all the rules for a healthy therapist/client relationship.** Start the clip immediately after Bob enters the elevator *(15 minutes into the video)* and end it when Bob and Dr. Marvin agree on a 4:00 p.m. phone meeting.

3) After watching the clip, ask your students to think of similar experiences when someone (or themselves) didn't play by the rules and what happened as a result. Have them share their stories aloud.

4) If you are unable to get the video, ask students to describe different situations where it really bothers them when people don't play by the rules. For example, the person who drives on the shoulder in the middle of a traffic tie-up. Continue with the discussion in question three, encouraging students to give specific examples.

**Preview this clip carefully to make sure you feel it is appropriate for your group. If you don't feel it is appropriate, substitute another video or other activity.*

Participation (10-15 minutes)

The exercise in this section is designed to frustrate your students as they experience what it's like to be on the receiving end of someone who plays by his or her own rules.

1) Announce that you're going to play a quick game of cards.

2) Give one deck of cards to each group of eight to ten students. If your group is ten students or less, stay in one group.

3) If you have more than one group, choose and prepare a leader for each group ahead of time. Take your leaders aside, and inform them that they may change the rules of the game whenever it's their turn. None of the other students will know this little rule.

4) Explain the game, using the following directions:

> a) The winner of the game is the first person to get rid of all his or her cards (the game is played similar to Crazy Eights).
>
> b) The leader begins play by laying down any card he or she wants.
>
> c) Going around the circle, the next person must lay down a card that is either from the same suit (spades, hearts, diamonds, or clubs) or is the same number as the last card played. For example: If you played the seven of hearts, the next person would need to lay down either a seven of any suit or another heart of any number.
>
> d) If the player doesn't have one of these cards in his or her hand, he or she must keep drawing cards from the deck until he or she gets a card that can be played.
>
> e) Each person may play only one card at a time.

5) When it's the leader's turn, he or she should change the rules so he or she will be able to play a card every time. Obviously, this will give the leader an unfair advantage—but that's the point of the game.

> Here's an example for the leader: Even if you have a proper card to play, lay down a wrong card, and then make up a new rule. You could say, **From now on, whenever someone plays a two, it's really a seven.** Lay your seven over the two that has been played. Be creative with your rule changing.

Do whatever you (and the other leaders) need to do to create an unfair advantage so you can win the game. When the students complain (and they will!), simply say you are the leader of the game and you have the right to change the rules whenever you wish.

Try to change the rules at least three or four times to ensure that you win the game. (The whole game shouldn't take more than 3-4 minutes.) After the game has finished, claim the prize and declare yourself the champion whether or not you actually won.

6) Bring your group of now-screaming students and victorious leaders back together. Your students will probably be quick to point out that the games weren't fair, because the leaders kept changing the rules to their advantage. Respond by saying, **Well, we really liked the prizes and wanted to make sure we won them.** Award yourselves the prizes.

Instruction (5-10 minutes)

This section helps your students understand that Jesus played by human rules when He could have easily changed the rules to ensure His victory.

1) Start by saying, **The card game wasn't fair because the leader(s) had a huge advantage over the players. It wasn't much fun and it caused tension in the groups.**

2) Then say, **I want to read you a story about the time Satan tempted Jesus. As I read the story, think about how Jesus reacted as a human being even though He could have used His supernatural powers as God to zap Satan.**

3) Read Matthew 4:1-11, and then make the following observations:

> a) Jesus experienced incredible temptations, but He played according to the rules God established. Jesus gave up His place with God to become human.
>
> b) By doing this, Jesus Himself was in a position to face the same kinds of temptations that we might face.
>
> c) Although Jesus was fully human and faced every temptation common to humanity, He was also fully God and never gave in to temptation and never sinned.

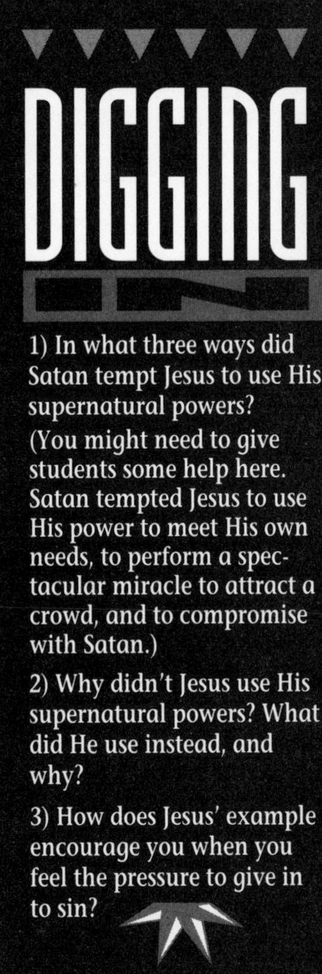

DIGGING IN
1) In what three ways did Satan tempt Jesus to use His supernatural powers?
(You might need to give students some help here. Satan tempted Jesus to use His power to meet His own needs, to perform a spectacular miracle to attract a crowd, and to compromise with Satan.)
2) Why didn't Jesus use His supernatural powers? What did He use instead, and why?
3) How does Jesus' example encourage you when you feel the pressure to give in to sin?

Observation (10 minutes)

This section helps your students to see, in a creative way, the truth that Jesus was once a teenager and fully human.

1) Hand out copies of *The Seven Ps of Puberty* (page 31) and spend a couple minutes explaining the typical "Ps" of teenage puberty. Depending on your group's mood, have fun with the descriptions so the students are drawn deeper into the illustrations.

2) After going through *The Seven Ps of Puberty*, show the drawing of *Jesus as a Teen* (page 32) that also expresses the "Ps" of puberty. This illustration

ought to provide your students with an "Ah ha!" feeling as they realize just how human Jesus really was. (If possible, photocopy these handouts onto a transparency and use them with an overhead projector. You'll have a little more control of when students see your main point. If you use the handouts, give them to students on two separate sheets of paper so they don't immediately make the connection and so that you have more time to set up Jesus' humanity.)

Application (5 minutes)
This section provides your students with another biblical passage that talks about the humanity of Jesus as well as a reminder that Jesus chose to become one of us.

1) Read this paraphrased version of Hebrews 4:15:

> **Because of Jesus' willingness to play by the rules, to become fully human, and to face every temptation we will ever face, we have a Savior who understands our struggles. But because He never sinned, we also have a Savior who paid the price for our sin.**

2) Give each student a playing card to take home. If you have the time, have the students write the Hebrews verse on their playing card. Encourage students to use the cards as reminders that Jesus was God and could have played by His own rules, but He wanted to relate to us and our struggles, so He became one of us and played by human rules so we would benefit and be eternal winners.

The Seven Ps of Puberty

CHRIS SCHMALTZ

Jesus as a Teen

CHRIS SCHMALTZ

LESSON THREE

JESUS AS HEALER

MARK 2:1-12

MATERIALS NEEDED

- Copies of *Amazing Medicals* (page 36)
- Medical awards (Band-Aids, Pepto-Bismol, ankle wrap)
- Pen and pad of paper
- Peanut butter, jelly, bread, kitchen knife
- Copies of *Personal Injury Report* (page 37)

Overview
This lesson is designed to help students understand that Jesus' healing power wasn't limited to His time on earth. Jesus' healing power is available today—for both spiritual and physical healing. (Note: You may want to adapt this lesson if you have a seriously ill or disabled student in your youth group. This lesson can still work, but you will need to handle it with care and sensitivity. Be prepared to answer questions about why God hasn't physically healed that particular student.)

Introduction (5-10 minutes)
This section gets your students thinking about illness in a lighthearted manner.

1) Pass out copies of *Amazing Medicals* (page 36) and give students time to circle their answers.

2) After a few minutes, read the correct answers and reward the winner(s) with a box of Band-Aids, an ankle wrap, a bottle of Pepto-Bismol or Kaopectate, or some other silly gift related to disease, injury, or sickness. The correct answers are: 1) b; 2) a; 3) c; 4) b; 5) b; 6) a; 7) a; 8) b; 9) b; 10) a.

Participation (10-15 minutes)
These exercises allow your group to feel a little uncomfortable watching someone struggle with a simple task. The intention is that students begin to think about how fortunate they are to have physical health.

You can do one or both of the following exercises, depending on your time and your students' participation. Exercise 1 works better with a small group, and Exercise 2 is easier to facilitate and observe in a large-group setting.

Exercise 1: Select a student volunteer. Have that student remove his or her shoes and socks and sit on the floor. Place a Bible on the floor, opened to Mark 2:1-12, give the student a pen and pad of paper, and instruct him or her to write the passage from Mark 2:1-12 using only his or her feet. You can increase the level of difficulty of this task by having the student keep his or her hands behind his or her back.

Exercise 2: Blindfold a student volunteer and guide him or her to a specific spot in the meeting room. Spin the student around until he or she is disoriented, and then instruct him or her to find his or her way to another place in the room.

Observation (5 minutes)

This section allows your students to watch you struggle with a simple task. It's also intended as a hook into the instruction time.

1) Tie your dominant hand behind your back.

2) Stand behind a table that has been set with the peanut butter, jelly, bread, and kitchen knife. Make a comment about fixing yourself a snack to maintain your energy level.

3) Attempt to make the sandwich with your opposite hand.

4) As you struggle to make the sandwich, begin the instruction phase.

Instruction (15 minutes)

This section teaches your students that Jesus heals both physically and spiritually.

1) Remind your students how privileged you all are to have working capacity of your bodies. You might say, **Many of us can't relate to struggling over simple tasks, like making a sandwich. We tend to take a lot for granted. I want to read a story about a disabled man and his encounter with Jesus.** By the way, when you've finished making the peanut butter sandwich, go ahead and eat it; then untie your hand.

2) Read aloud Mark 2:1-12.

3) Then say, **There are a few quick observations I'd like to make about this story:**

> **a) This man's healing started with forgiveness (verse 5).**

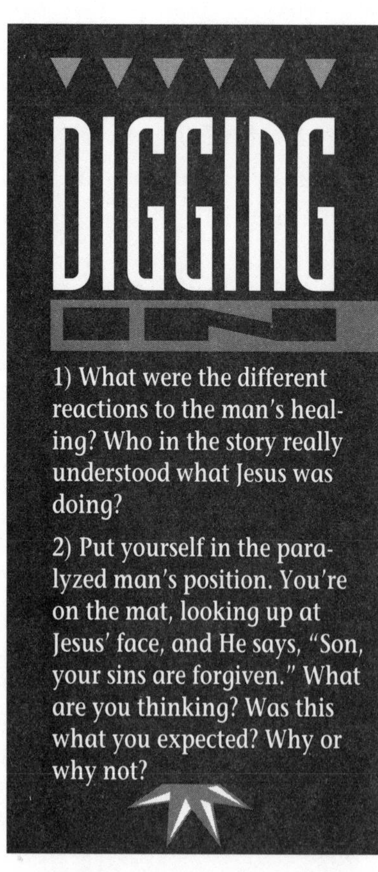

DIGGING
IN
1) What were the different reactions to the man's healing? Who in the story really understood what Jesus was doing?
2) Put yourself in the paralyzed man's position. You're on the mat, looking up at Jesus' face, and He says, "Son, your sins are forgiven." What are you thinking? Was this what you expected? Why or why not?

b) This man's injury didn't keep him from seeking Jesus (verses 2-4).

c) This man had great friends who played a role in his healing (verse 3).

4) Ask your students to share other things they observed about the story.

Application (5-10 minutes)
This section helps your students think of ways to apply the main observations about the paralytic in Mark 2:1-12.

1) Explain to the students that you'd like them to check their own lives for specific "injuries." Challenge them to think not only about physical injuries, but also about emotional or spiritual injuries—injuries that might require forgiveness, personal healing, or healing in their relationships. Pass out copies of the *Personal Injury Report* (page 37).

2) Have your students fill out the *Personal Injury Report*. Encourage them to follow through on sharing what they write down with a friend.*

*If you feel it is appropriate, let your students know that you are also available to talk. If you make this option available, make a list of several professional counselors and therapists for referrals in case you are told about an "injury" that requires more professional help than you are equipped to provide.

Be aware of the reporting requirements stipulated by law in case of physical or sexual abuse, the potential for suicide, or other reportable issues.

AMAZING MEDICALS

MY STRABISMUS IS KILLIN' ME!

1) A poroxythemetic is:
- a) a broken arm
- b) a shattered tendon
- c) a hemorrhoid
- d) a strained eyelash

2) A tachycardia is:
- a) a rapid heartbeat
- b) a weakness of the vein walls
- c) a chronic hangnail inflammation
- d) a substance or condition normally harmless

3) A chilblain is:
- a) a weight control problem
- b) trouble falling asleep
- c) a skin rash due to exposure to cold
- d) a red and puffy eyeball

4) A myringotomy is:
- a) an enriched nutritional deficiency
- b) a lumpy deposit in the spleen
- c) small opening in the eardrum
- d) disordered development of speech

5) A lipoma is:
- a) an omatic inflammation of the lips
- b) a benign tumor composed of fat cells
- c) shriveled epidermis
- d) overactive elbow expenditure

6) A myopia is:
- a) nearsightedness
- b) disorientation of simple discomfort
- c) degenerative porousness of the blood
- d) inflamed freckle

7) A strabismus is:
- a) crossed eyes
- b) infection of the middle ear
- c) symptomatic indication
- d) severe local aggression

8) A phlebitis is:
- a) throat mucus
- b) inflammation of the veins
- c) blood clot within vessels
- d) runny nose

9) A sphygmomanometer is:
- a) a device to measure the strength of a hair follicle
- b) a device to take blood pressure
- c) a device used in AIDS testing
- d) a device to measure the sensory neuron in a spinal column

10) Subcutaneous is:
- a) a layer of fatty tissue below the dermis
- b) oil that seeps through pimple wall
- c) a weak pigment in the skin
- d) a strong pygmy in Africa

I. THE MAN'S HEALING STARTED WITH FORGIVENESS

List three areas of your life where you need forgiveness or need to forgive someone.

1.

2.

3.

II. THE MAN'S INJURY DIDN'T KEEP HIM FROM SEEKING JESUS

Circle the injured area that best represents your present injuries or struggles. Next to it, list some ideas you have that might help your injury.

1. My head (things I think about)

2. My heart (how I feel)

3. My mouth (things I say)

4. My feet (places I go)

5. My hands (things I do)

III. THIS MAN HAD GREAT FRIENDS WHO PLAYED A ROLE IN HIS HEALING

Who is one friend you can share your injury with?

Confess your sins to each other and pray for each other so that you may be healed.
The prayer of a righteous man is powerful and effective.
James 5:16

LESSON FOUR

JESUS AS SALVAGER

JOHN 4:1-42

MATERIALS NEEDED

- Play dough, modeling clay, or chewing gum
- Copies of *Insurance Destruction Report* (page 42)
- Prizes for best creative reason
- Several destroyed objects
- Copies of phony labels (page 43)
- Dishwashing liquid
- Two plastic bottles
- Dirty dishes in a sink (possibly in your church kitchen)
- Water
- Copies of *Personal Brokenness Report* (page 44)

Overview

This lesson is designed to help students see that Jesus can salvage and restore the brokenness in their lives.

Introduction (10-15 minutes)

This section introduces the theme of making something from "nothing."

1) Provide your students with some play dough, modeling clay, or chewing gum.

2) Have students split into groups of three to five and make some type of sculpture from the clay or gum. Inform them that the goal for each group is to make something from "nothing."

3) When they finish, have each group share and explain its masterpiece to the other groups.

Participation (10-15 minutes)

This section gets your students thinking about the results of destruction.

1) Provide each student or group of students with a destroyed object. These objects should be simple and easy to find around your church or home. Examples might include:

- piece of a broken mirror
- ripped paper cup
- aluminum can ripped in half
- broken chair leg

2) Hand out a copy of *Insurance Destruction Report* (page 42) to each student.

3) Have each student fill out the report, using his or her destroyed object as the source for information. Each student will need to explain why the object can't be repaired and why he or she should be rewarded with a new item (see question 7 on report).

4) Have your students share their reports. Award a prize for the most creative reason given for replacement.

Observation (10-15 minutes)
This section uses a concrete example of cleansing (that is, washing dishes) to help students understand how God cleanses us from sin with His living water.

1) Before your meeting, copy the two phony labels titled "Water" and "Living Water Salvage System" (page 43).

2) Cut out the labels and attach them to two different empty plastic squeeze bottles.

3) The bottle with the "Water" label should be filled with water.

4) The label "Living Water Salvage System" should be attached to a bottle filled with dishwashing liquid.

5) Take your students to a sink that you filled with a stack of dirty dishes. If you don't have access to a sink, bring in a couple of buckets filled with water, and a stack of dirty dishes from home. (If you take the group to the church kitchen, you'll also need to bring your Bible with you to read this lesson's passage.) Attempt to clean the dirty dishes using only the Water. Make sure the dishes are dirty and crusted enough so that the water won't do a complete cleaning job.

6) Display the dishes and allow the students to see that water alone isn't strong enough for the job. Then complete the washing job with the Living Water Salvage System.

7) Explain to the students that you're not exactly sure what's in the bottle, but there's something significant about the Living Water.

8) As you wash the dishes, open your Bible to John 4:1-42 and read it aloud. Be ready to teach once you've finished reading. It doesn't really matter if you've finished washing all the dishes. The students' focus will be changed, you're ready to teach, so you can take your group back to the

meeting room and forget about the dishes.

Instruction (5-10 minutes)
This section helps your students understand that only Jesus can change and salvage lives.

1) When everyone has settled down, say, **The Scripture I just read teaches us a few things about Jesus that only He can do. Jesus is in the salvage business, and only He can**

> **a) clean our dirty lives and restore us from true brokenness;**
>
> **b) make something significant out of what is insignificant;**
>
> **c) change our lives.**

2) Give your students an opportunity to share any other things they noticed about the story.

Application (5-10 minutes)
This section gives your students a chance to reflect on their personal brokenness and to ask Jesus to be a part of their restoration and healing.

1) Hand out the *Personal Brokenness Report* (page 44).

2) Have each student fill out the report. Encourage kids to reread their reports within the next twenty-four hours and pray specifically for the help they need that only God can provide.

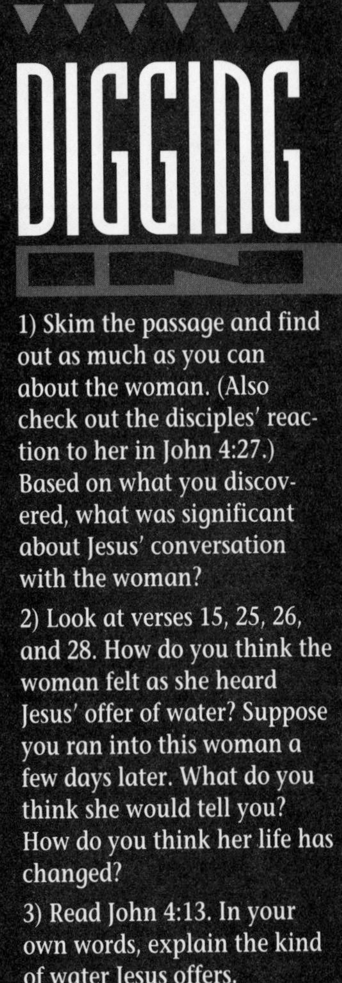

DIGGING IN

1) Skim the passage and find out as much as you can about the woman. (Also check out the disciples' reaction to her in John 4:27.) Based on what you discovered, what was significant about Jesus' conversation with the woman?

2) Look at verses 15, 25, 26, and 28. How do you think the woman felt as she heard Jesus' offer of water? Suppose you ran into this woman a few days later. What do you think she would tell you? How do you think her life has changed?

3) Read John 4:13. In your own words, explain the kind of water Jesus offers.

Insurance DESTRUCTION report

1) Describe your destroyed item.____

2) What was the item's purpose?____

3) Is this item presently functional?____

4) Can it ever be completely restored? *(If your answer is yes, skip to question 6.)*________________

5) Is there anything that can be salvaged from this item in its present condition?____________

6) What would it take to restore this item to new?____

7) Why should you be rewarded with a new item?____

WATER

Living
Water
Salvage
System

Personal BROKENNESS report

1) Explain your purpose for living.

2) What is one area of your life that appears to be broken?

3) Is your brokenness keeping you from fulfilling your purpose for living? *(If yes, provide a specific example.)*

4) What would you like God to do about your brokenness? *(Ask God in a specific manner before you go to bed tonight.)*

5) What can others learn from your brokenness?

. . . that you and I may be mutually encouraged by each other's faith.
Romans 1:12

LESSON FIVE

JESUS AS CONFRONTER

LUKE 4:28-30; JOHN 8:3-11; JOHN 2:13-16

MATERIALS NEEDED

- Copies of *What Would it Take?* (page 48)
- "Spots" to identify conflict cycles (rings from a ring toss game or Hula Hoops could work well—see page 49)
- A copy of *Six Stages of Conflict,* with each stage cut apart (page 50)
- Copy of *Arguing Student Script* (page 51)
- Copies of *Conflict Business Card* (page 52)

Overview

This lesson is designed to help students see that conflict and confrontation are a normal part of life even among Christians. It focuses on conflict and provides them with a tool to help resolve conflict. This lesson also helps them see how Jesus handled conflict and how He confronted the sin that kept people's eyes from God.

Introduction (5-10 minutes)

This section gets your students thinking about their ability to confront, their willingness to confront, and their response to confrontation.

1) Give each student a copy of the handout titled *What Would It Take?* (page 48).

2) Have your students record their thoughts.

3) Have your students share briefly what would be the hardest areas for them to confront from the items listed on *What Would It Take?*

Participation (10-15 minutes)

This section provides your students with a model they can use in resolving conflict.

1) Place six circular spots or marks on the floor in the form of a circle (see page 49). As you do so, say something like this: **Just because you confront someone doesn't automatically mean you've resolved the conflict. In fact, how you confront someone and what you say goes a long way in resolving conflict.**

2) Continue with an explanation of the six spots. **Each of these six spots represents one stage of the conflict cycle:**

- **Stage 1: Tension**
- **Stage 2: Asking Questions**
- **Stage 3: Gathering Ammunition**
- **Stage 4: Confrontation**
- **Stage 5: Making Adjustments**
- **Stage 6: Resolution**

3) Split your students equally among each of the six spots. Ask groups to sit down around their spots.

4) Hand each group the strip from the handout *Six Stages of Conflict* (page 50) that defines the stage it's sitting at.

5) Have one student at each stage read the definition on the strip to his or her group.

6) Have each group come up with a real-life example that illustrates its particular stage. If groups need help getting started, here's an example for Stage 2: Asking Questions. Katie missed her curfew a few times in a row, and now her mom won't let her go to the concert Friday night. Katie is furious. True, missing curfew—without calling— is a pretty big deal, so maybe her mom has a right to be angry, but she never said anything about being grounded. So why is Katie so angry? She thinks her mom is overreacting and isn't being very fair.

7) Before groups have finished giving input and illustrations, move into the observation section.

Observation (5-10 minutes)

This section helps your students to see the conflict model put into action.

As groups are still sharing, have a student begin an argument with you. You'll need to choose the "arguing" student before the meeting and give him or her a copy of the script on page 51. The script is a guide for the staged conflict. It doesn't need to be memorized, but you and the student should know it well enough to carry out the argument as naturally as possible. When you've finished the "argument," gather everyone back together and briefly explain what you just did and why (you just gave your groups an eyewitness glimpse into the stages, and resolution, of a conflict).

Instruction (10-15 minutes)

This section introduces the Scriptures for this lesson and helps your students to see that Jesus was familiar with conflict. He confronted the things that took people's eyes off of God.

1) Say, **I wanted you to see a model of resolving conflict you can use when you encounter conflict. I also want you to see how Jesus handled conflict and confrontation.**

2) Then say, **The Bible shows us specific instances where Jesus was involved with conflict. I want us to take a look at three of them.** (If you have the time, look briefly at all three examples. If you don't have enough time, mention A and B, then focus on C—Jesus started conflict.)

a) Jesus avoided conflict (read Luke 4:28-30)
b) Jesus resolved conflict (read John 8:3-11)
c) Jesus started conflict (read John 2:13-16)

3) After reading the passage in John 2, say, **The big idea from this Scripture is that Jesus confronted a situation that took people's eyes away from God. Jesus wants you to confront those same issues.** Ask your students to suggest specific examples of what those issues might include. (Have your students refer back to *What Would It Take?* for ideas.)

Application (5 minutes)

This section will give students a tool to help them remember the conflict cycle, and remind them that Jesus wants them to confront areas in their lives where they take their eyes off of God.

1) Pass out copies of the *Conflict Business Card* (page 52) to every student. Encourage them to keep the card with them, and refer to the card when they find themselves in a conflict situation.

2) If possible, copy the cards on to heavy paper stock before you pass them out. They will last longer in a wallet or purse.

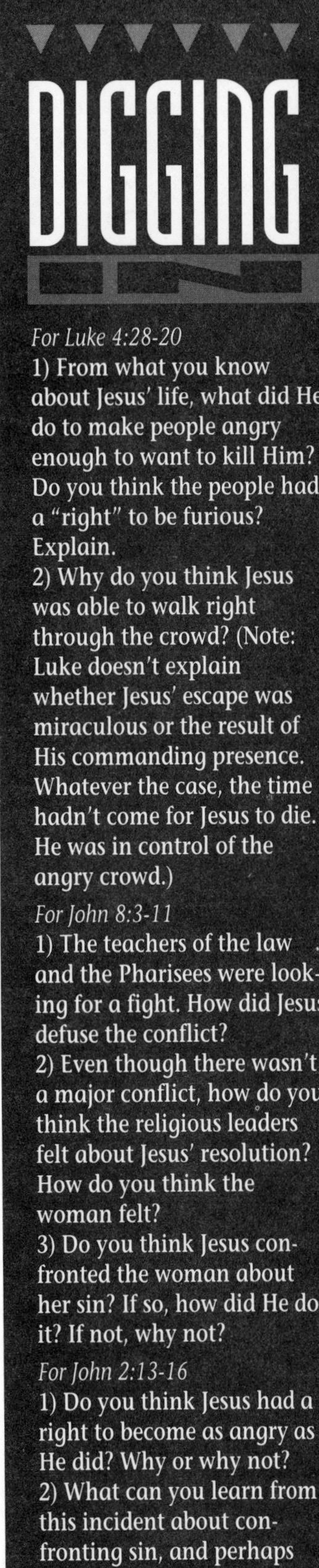

DIGGING IN

For Luke 4:28-20
1) From what you know about Jesus' life, what did He do to make people angry enough to want to kill Him? Do you think the people had a "right" to be furious? Explain.
2) Why do you think Jesus was able to walk right through the crowd? (Note: Luke doesn't explain whether Jesus' escape was miraculous or the result of His commanding presence. Whatever the case, the time hadn't come for Jesus to die. He was in control of the angry crowd.)

For John 8:3-11
1) The teachers of the law and the Pharisees were looking for a fight. How did Jesus defuse the conflict?
2) Even though there wasn't a major conflict, how do you think the religious leaders felt about Jesus' resolution? How do you think the woman felt?
3) Do you think Jesus confronted the woman about her sin? If so, how did He do it? If not, why not?

For John 2:13-16
1) Do you think Jesus had a right to become as angry as He did? Why or why not?
2) What can you learn from this incident about confronting sin, and perhaps creating conflict between you and someone else?

What would it take for you to confront your good friends? Below is a list of things your friends might do someday. Place an (!) next to the actions you would confront immediately. Place a (+) next to the ones that you might confront. And place a (-) next to the activities you would not confront.

- Cheating in school
- Stealing money from parents
- Spreading rumors
- Drinking and driving
- Bingeing and purging
- Using drugs
- Having sex
- Bad-mouthing the youth pastor
- Planning to have an abortion
- Being involved in Satanism
- Selling drugs
- Lying to friends
- Making fun of one of your friends

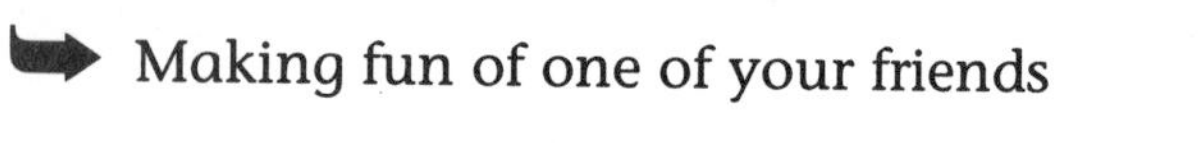

Do you have a system for confronting and resolving conflict?

yes   no

If yes, describe your system:

CONFLICT CYCLE

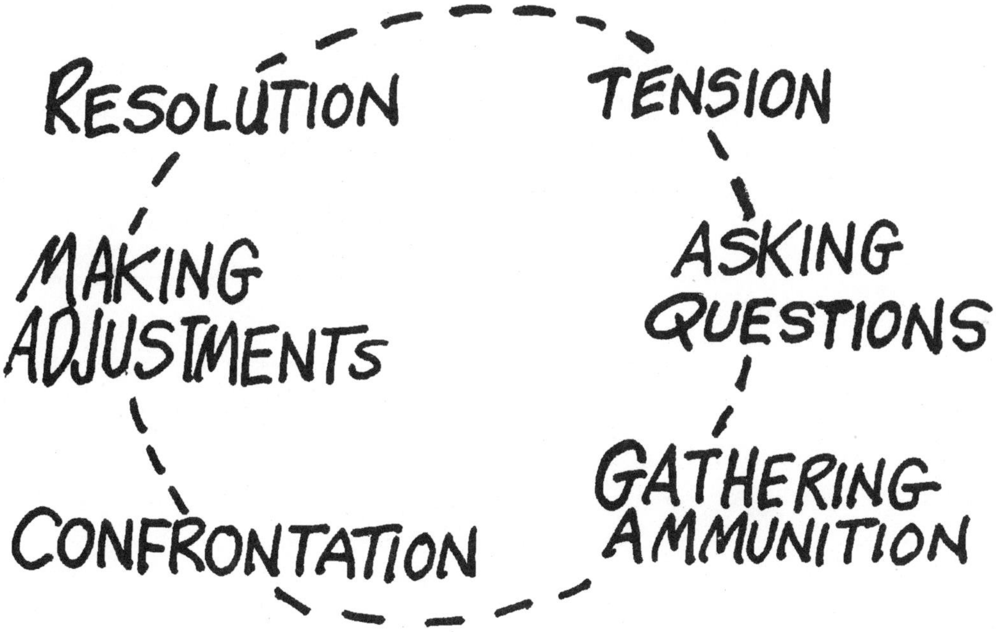

RESOLUTION

TENSION

ASKING QUESTIONS

GATHERING AMMUNITION

CONFRONTATION

MAKING ADJUSTMENTS

SIX STAGES OF CONFLICT

STAGE 1: TENSION

All conflicts have a beginning. This is where you first experience feelings of tension and know that there is some type of friction between you and the other person. At this point, your feelings come into play and you may feel angry, hurt, betrayed, or misunderstood.

STAGE 2: ASKING QUESTIONS

This is where you begin to ask yourself questions such as “Is this my fault?” “Do I have the right to be feeling this way?” “What did I do to deserve this?” You are trying to figure out why you feel the way you do. This is the best stage to attempt to resolve your conflict. Ask the questions you’ve been asking yourself to the person or parties with which you have conflict. Do it right away, and you can skip stage three.

STAGE 3: GATHERING AMMUNITION

This is the stage where anger takes over, and you begin to think of ways to put the other person down or get even with him or her. This stage is dangerous and should be avoided whenever possible. If you get stuck at this stage, the next stage can become a battleground.

STAGE 4: CONFRONTATION

This is the vital stage in the conflict cycle. Confrontation involves spending time with the other person(s), talking about the conflict. It’s best to do this in a sensitive manner, with both sides getting the chance to express and explain their feelings. If there has been a lot of ammunition built up going into this stage, the confrontation can be painful, difficult, and counterproductive.

STAGE 5: MAKING ADJUSTMENTS

If the confrontation stage is managed well, you can then make adjustments to improve the relationship. Both parties need to agree on the changes and talk about specific expectations, so the tensions can begin to diminish. It’s best for both parties to do some changing and work as a team in bringing resolution.

STAGE 6: RESOLUTION

The conflict is finally over and your life is moving back toward normalcy. It doesn’t mean the pain will be over—especially if you felt hurt in the tension—but it means you are moving toward forgiveness and getting on with your life.

ARGUING STUDENT SCRIPT

Student—**S** (let's call her Sharon for example only)
Leader—**L**

S: (*Interrupting another student in mid-sentence*) That's a stupid example. Someone must have a better one.

L: Sharon, let's not be critical of the other group's illustration at this point. Let's just listen.

S: I don't think it has anything to do with the topic. They're way out of it.

L: If you let them finish, it may make more sense to you.

S: Just put me down, why don't you. I hate it when you do that!

L: Do what?

S: You always cut me down in front of the others. You don't like me.

L: You're catching me off guard, Sharon. I didn't know you felt that way.

S: Well, I do feel that way and you always put me down! You treat me like I don't have anything important to say.

L: To be honest, I don't like it when you interrupt people all the time. I simply try to get the conversation going again. I don't do it to hurt your feelings.

S: Well, I just want to say what I feel, but you always tell me to wait or that it's not my turn. It makes me pretty mad!

L: I'm sorry.

S: You could have been up-front with me after one of our meetings so I wouldn't think you didn't like me. Just be direct with me next time.

L: You are right, Sharon. I should have done that. I am sorry. I promise I'll do that from now on.

S: Okay. I'll try to avoid interrupting people and wait my turn to talk.

L: Great! Sorry to make you so angry.

S: Yeah, me too!

CONFLICT BUSINESS CARD

Stage	*Description of Stage*	*Key Words*
1	Tension	Conflict begins
2	Asking Questions	Why did this happen
3	Gathering Ammunition	I hate . . . (try to skip)
4	Confrontation	Let's talk
5	Making Adjustments	What should we do now
6	Resolution	Forgive and move on

Do not let the sun go down while you are still angry.
Ephesians 4:26

Stage	*Description of Stage*	*Key Words*
1	Tension	Conflict begins
2	Asking Questions	Why did this happen
3	Gathering Ammunition	I hate . . . (try to skip)
4	Confrontation	Let's talk
5	Making Adjustments	What should we do now
6	Resolution	Forgive and move on

Do not let the sun go down while you are still angry.
Ephesians 4:26

Stage	*Description of Stage*	*Key Words*
1	Tension	Conflict begins
2	Asking Questions	Why did this happen
3	Gathering Ammunition	I hate . . . (try to skip)
4	Confrontation	Let's talk
5	Making Adjustments	What should we do now
6	Resolution	Forgive and move on

Do not let the sun go down while you are still angry.
Ephesians 4:26

Stage	*Description of Stage*	*Key Words*
1	Tension	Conflict begins
2	Asking Questions	Why did this happen
3	Gathering Ammunition	I hate . . . (try to skip)
4	Confrontation	Let's talk
5	Making Adjustments	What should we do now
6	Resolution	Forgive and move on

Do not let the sun go down while you are still angry.
Ephesians 4:26

Stage	*Description of Stage*	*Key Words*
1	Tension	Conflict begins
2	Asking Questions	Why did this happen
3	Gathering Ammunition	I hate . . . (try to skip)
4	Confrontation	Let's talk
5	Making Adjustments	What should we do now
6	Resolution	Forgive and move on

Do not let the sun go down while you are still angry.
Ephesians 4:26

Stage	*Description of Stage*	*Key Words*
1	Tension	Conflict begins
2	Asking Questions	Why did this happen
3	Gathering Ammunition	I hate . . . (try to skip)
4	Confrontation	Let's talk
5	Making Adjustments	What should we do now
6	Resolution	Forgive and move on

Do not let the sun go down while you are still angry.
Ephesians 4:26

Stage	*Description of Stage*	*Key Words*
1	Tension	Conflict begins
2	Asking Questions	Why did this happen
3	Gathering Ammunition	I hate . . . (try to skip)
4	Confrontation	Let's talk
5	Making Adjustments	What should we do now
6	Resolution	Forgive and move on

Do not let the sun go down while you are still angry.
Ephesians 4:26

Stage	*Description of Stage*	*Key Words*
1	Tension	Conflict begins
2	Asking Questions	Why did this happen
3	Gathering Ammunition	I hate . . . (try to skip)
4	Confrontation	Let's talk
5	Making Adjustments	What should we do now
6	Resolution	Forgive and move on

Do not let the sun go down while you are still angry.
Ephesians 4:26

LESSON SIX

JESUS AS SERVANT

JOHN 13:2-20

MATERIALS NEEDED

- Copy of *Mad Lib* (page 56)
- Vacuum cleaner
- Dust rags, dusters
- Cleaning supplies (buckets, cleaning solutions, rags, etc.)
- Water
- 3" x 5" cards
- Hat
- Pencils
- Chalk, chalkboard
- Copies of *Servanthood Hit List* (page 57)

Overview

This lesson is designed to show that Jesus was a servant and to challenge students to follow His example.

Introduction (5-10 minutes)

This section introduces the topic of servanthood with a humorous and light opener.

1) Explain to the students that they will be participating in a *Mad Lib* (page 56). Don't show them the *Mad Lib* sheet.

2) First, ask your students to call out the appropriate words or phrases you need to complete the *Mad Lib*. For example, ask them to give you a plural noun or a verb. Encourage the group to call out unusual and funny words. The more outlandish these words are, the more fun it is.

3) Don't allow your students to see the *Mad Lib* as you are filling in the blanks. The humor comes when you read the story aloud with the words students supplied.

4) When you've finished reading, say something like this: **Most people don't think of serving others as funny or fun. What do you think of when you hear the word "service"?**

Participation (10-15 minutes)
This section allows your students to perform simple and common acts of service.

1) Before the meeting, set up the vacuum cleaner, dust rags, and cleaning supplies. Have your students brainstorm different tasks of servanthood that they can perform right now in your meeting room (for example, vacuuming the carpet, rearranging furniture, dusting). You may need to come prepared with some of your own ideas of servanthood in case your students aren't familiar with the concept of serving. Be creative, but also provide ideas that you would like to see happen on a regular basis.

2) Write all of the servanthood ideas on 3" x 5" cards, one card for each idea.

3) Place the cards in a hat and allow each student to draw a card.

4) Then have each student or team of students perform the task he or she drew from the hat. Be prepared for some grumbling and complaining. Reassure the students that this is part of the lesson.

5) After your students complete their tasks, have them write their feelings about doing an unexpected act of servanthood on a chalkboard, whiteboard, or easel. Have them explain why they felt the way they did.

Observation (5-10 minutes)
This section gets your students thinking about the people they would feel comfortable serving, and those they wouldn't feel comfortable serving.

1) Ask your students to come up with a list of people whom they know personally or know by name only (the list might include celebrities, parents, friends, teachers).

2) After you have compiled a list, go through it and have the students determine the people on the list who would be easy to serve and who would not. Ask the students why they would or would not want to serve each person listed.

3) See if you can establish any similarities or patterns in their choices. For example: **Isn't it interesting that most of us in here would find it easier to serve people we don't know than people we do know, like our family and friends?**

4) Then say, **I'd like to read a story about the greatest person who ever lived. Listen and try to understand why He said what He said about servanthood.**

Instruction (10-15 minutes)
This session allows your students to see Jesus' example of servanthood and the priority He placed on living out His commitment to serve others.

1) Read John 13:2-20. During the reading of this passage, you may want to have one student wash another student's feet to serve as a visual aid. Explain what you're doing beforehand, so the foot washing enhances, not detracts from, the story.

2) This story illustrates a profound truth students need to understand. You might say, **Sometimes it's difficult to know how to serve one another. In this story, we see Jesus' example of servanthood when He washed the disciple's feet.**

3) Then say, **If we are to follow the example of Jesus, we must understand that servanthood means**

> **a) putting others first;**
> **b) putting aside our pride;**
> **c) participating in an active way.**

Application (5 minutes)
This session provides your students with an opportunity to personalize the concept of servanthood.

1) Hand out pencils and copies of *Servanthood Hit List* (page 57) to every student.

2) Have your students create their own "Servanthood Hit List" by listing five people they can serve this week.

3) Instruct students to write down one realistic way that they can serve each person on their list. Challenge them to follow through and do what they wrote on their list.

4) Emphasize to your students that they are never more like Christ than when they serve others.

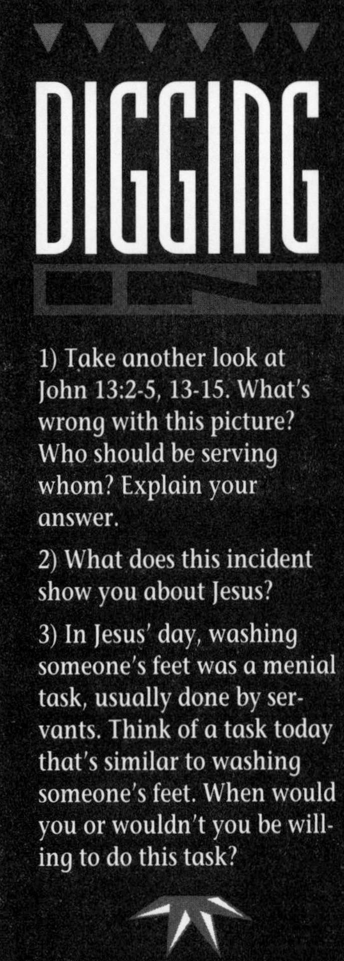

DIGGING
IN
1) Take another look at John 13:2-5, 13-15. What's wrong with this picture? Who should be serving whom? Explain your answer.
2) What does this incident show you about Jesus?
3) In Jesus' day, washing someone's feet was a menial task, usually done by servants. Think of a task today that's similar to washing someone's feet. When would you or wouldn't you be willing to do this task?

WAYS TO SERVE

If you would like to be a servant, you must first learn how to__________(verb). ___________ (person's name) is a great example of a servant. He or she always takes__________(plural noun) and __________(plural noun) and puts them in __________(place) for security. A person can also serve by __________(verb ending in "ing") a __________(noun) or __________(adverb) doing __________(adjective) chores for ____________(person's name). One of the true marks of a servant is the ability to ___________(verb) on command and to__________(adverb) produce both __________(plural noun) or __________(plural noun). Another wonderful way to serve is to go through___________(a period in life) thinking that you are a __________ (an animal). This will help you to __________(verb) better than the average __________(noun). Finally, you must always keep this motto in mind: If you want to serve, you must ____________(verb) ___________(plural noun) and never forget to __________(verb) your ___________(noun). Most importantly, you should always serve others by constantly shouting,"__________________ (a favorite saying or quote)."

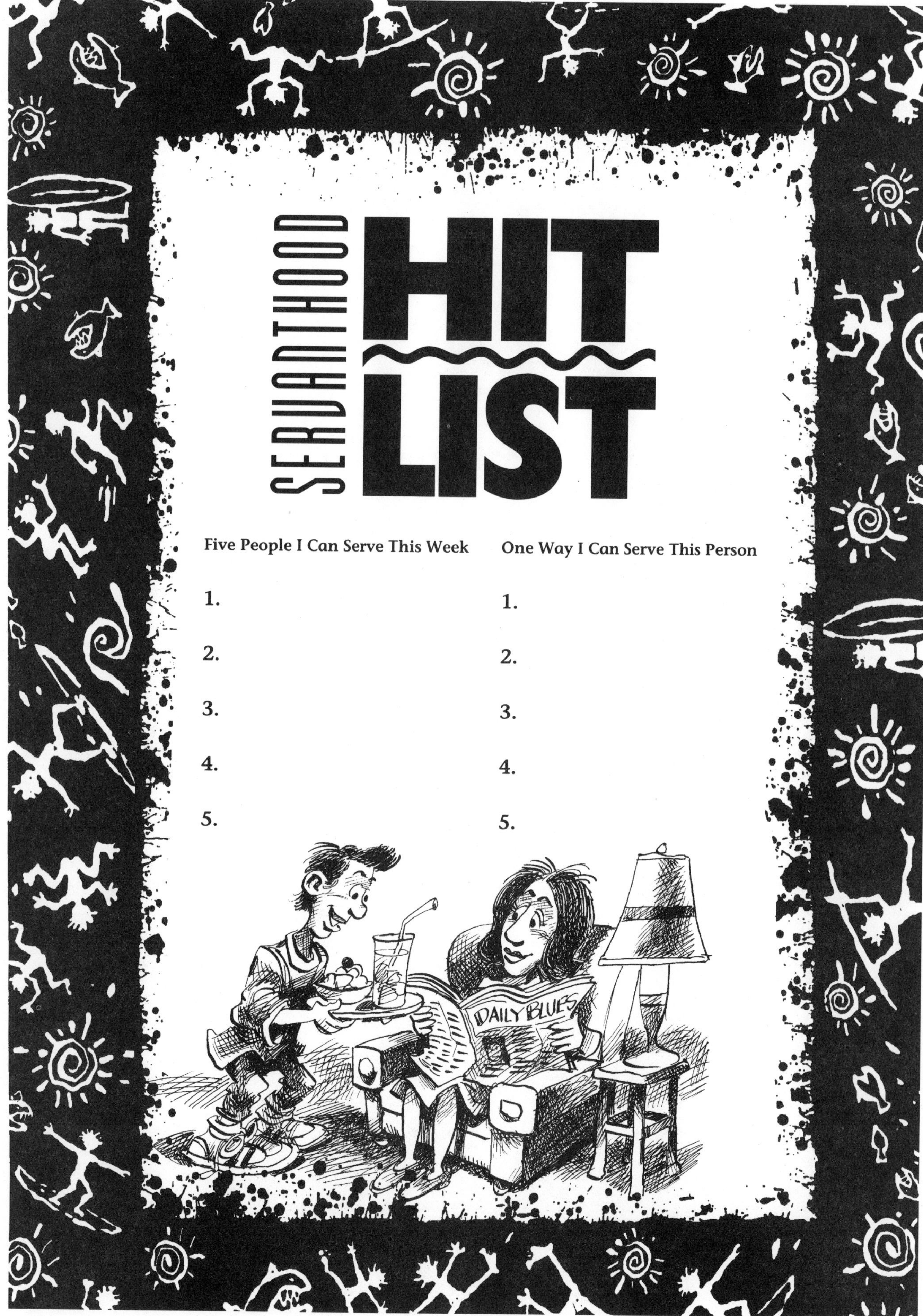

SERVANTHOOD HIT LIST

Five People I Can Serve This Week	One Way I Can Serve This Person
1.	1.
2.	2.
3.	3.
4.	4.
5.	5.

LESSON SEVEN

JESUS AS SHEPHERD

JOHN 10:11-18

MATERIALS NEEDED

- A copy of *Top 10 Things a Shepherd Would Never Say to a Sheep* (page 63)
- Chalkboard, large sheet of construction paper, or butcher paper
- Partial drawing of sheep (page 64)
- Colored chalk or wide felt pens in different colors
- Three blindfolds
- Dual-cassette tape deck with high-speed dubbing feature (or reel-to-reel tape deck)
- Copies of *The Lord Is My Shepherd* (page 65)

Overview

This lesson is designed to give the students an understanding of Jesus as the Good Shepherd. It encourages them to find comfort in the fact that Jesus truly cares about their lives.
(**Note:** Before you begin this lesson, have your students share how well they did with their *Servanthood Hit Lists*. Celebrate any of their successes.)

Introduction (5 minutes)

This section is intended to be a humorous way of explaining the role of a shepherd and the shepherd's relationship to sheep.

1) Inform your students that you will be talking about shepherds and sheep.

2) Explain to your students that a shepherd's responsibility is to care for and watch over his sheep. Good shepherds make sure the sheep are treated well and stay alive.

3) Read the *Top 10 Things a Shepherd Would Never Say to a Sheep* (page 63). This is intended for a humorous opener. Remember that most humor is dependent on delivery and timing. If you feel uncomfortable with either of the two, you might photocopy the *Top 10* and hand it out, or use an overhead projector and unveil one sentence at a time.

4) As an option, let students come up with their own top ten lists to present to each other. Or ask your students to think of "baad" sheep jokes.

Participation (10-15 minutes)
This section gets your students moving and helps them to discover firsthand the benefit of having someone provide direction.

1) Before your meeting, draw a partial drawing of a sheep on a large piece of butcher paper or construction paper or the chalkboard (see the example on page 64).

2) If you used the butcher or construction paper, tape it to the wall. If you used the chalkboard, make sure students can see the board with your incomplete masterpiece on it.

3) Explain to your students that the goal of this activity is to complete the drawing of the sheep. The catch is that the students will be blindfolded.

4) Ask for three volunteers. Have them stand in the back of the room and take one last look at the drawing on the paper or chalkboard.

5) Blindfold them.

6) Give each volunteer a piece of colored chalk or a marker.

7) Tell them what part of the sheep you want each of them to draw.

8) As in the birthday party game "Pin the Tail on the Donkey," spin each student around a few times, and then have the person make his or her way to the chalkboard and draw the part of the sheep as accurately as he or she can. It's important that no one gives these students any direction.

9) When the volunteers have finished drawing, ask for one last volunteer. Allow this final student to have a partner, and refer to this partner as the shepherd.

10) Instruct the shepherd to guide the artist to a new drawing location and provide directions as to what and where to draw. Have this volunteer complete an entire sheep.

11) Your group will see the importance of the "shepherd" as they compare the results of the drawings done by the unguided volunteers with the drawings of the "shepherded" volunteer.

Observation (5 minutes)
This section sets up the main points of the instruction section.

1) Prior to the meeting, have several different students record portions of the Scripture passage, John 10:11-18, on a cassette tape at normal speed.

Record the verses in order, so when the tape is played back you will be able to understand the entire eight verses in John, chapter ten.

2) During the meeting, play the tape for your students at "high-speed dub" speed. In order to set up the instructional time, be sure the tape is so distorted that the sounds are more humorous than understandable. You don't want the students to be able to understand the recording.

3) As an option to the recording, choose three volunteers ahead of time to read John 10:11-18. Keep these students hidden behind a screen or a table turned on its end. You don't want the rest of the group to see them! At your signal, ask each volunteer to read the Scripture passage as quickly as possible and in his or her most disguised voice.

Instruction (10-15 minutes)
This section helps your students understand their personal relationship with Jesus as their shepherd.

1) Ask your students, **What would make the tape (or people) more understandable?** Write their answers on a chalkboard, so everyone can see the answers.

2) You will probably receive several different answers, but circle or highlight the three that are closest to the following:

a) Slow down the tape speed, or have the people read slowly.

b) Be there with the person while he or she is recording his or her part, or be able to see the people who are reading.

c) Know the person's voice so well that you could understand it at any speed, or no matter how well disguised the person's voice is.

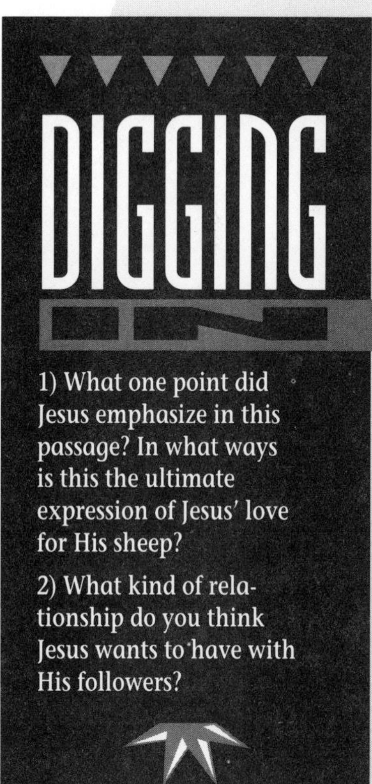

DIGGING
IN
1) What one point did Jesus emphasize in this passage? In what ways is this the ultimate expression of Jesus' love for His sheep?
2) What kind of relationship do you think Jesus wants to have with His followers?

3) Rewind the tape and play it at regular speed. The students should be able to clearly hear the reading of John 10:11-18. Or ask your volunteers to come out of hiding and read the passage clearly and distinctly.

4) Explain the parallels between understanding the tape and developing our understanding of God as our Shepherd. They are

a) getting "in sync" with God's will;

b) spending time with Him;

c) learning to recognize God's voice through Scripture, our conscience, and the wisdom of human "shepherds" God puts in our lives.

Application (5-10 minutes)

This section gets students to think through the analogy of a shepherd as they respond in specific ways to Psalm 23.

1) Pass out copies of *The Lord Is My Shepherd* (page 65) and blank paper for students to write down their responses.

2) Have your students read through the psalm and respond to the appropriate questions.

3) Have your students share some of their answers.

Top 10 Things a Shepherd Would Never Say to a Sheep

10) Who are ewe?

9) How much lamb could a lamb chop chop if a lamb chop could chop lamb?

8) Who wants mutton on their pizza?

7) I just don't understand why you guys don't shrink when it rains.

6) You're pulling the wool over my eyes.

5) Wolf! Wolf! Ha, ha, ha. I love scaring you guys. Your eyes get as big as quarters, I tell you.

4) Baa, baa black sheep have you any wool? Yes sir, yes sir, three bags full. Okay, second verse same as the first.

3) I've got two words for you: "wolf bait."

2) If you can't sleep, try counting people jumping over a fence.

1) Hey, cookie, can you fix us some lamb chops?

THE LORD IS MY SHEPHERD

Psalm 23

Verse 1: The Lord is my shepherd, I shall not be in want.
How has God provided for you recently?

Verse 2: He makes me lie down in green pastures, he leads me beside quiet waters.
Where can you go and spend quiet time with God to be calm, read His Word, and pray?

What area in your life is stormy, and you need God to calm the storm?

Verse 3: He restores my soul. He guides me in the paths of righteousness for his name's sake.
Is there something in your life that you know God probably isn't pleased with? What can you do to get on the right path?

Verse 4: Even though I walk through the valley of the shadow of death, I will fear no evil, for you are with me; your rod and your staff, they comfort me.
Do you remember a time when you were unsure or afraid and God brought you comfort? Describe that time.

Verse 5: You prepare a table before me in the presence of my enemies. You anoint my head with oil; my cup overflows.
What are some of the good things God has given you or done for you?

Verse 6: Surely goodness and love will follow me all the days of my life, and I will dwell in the house of the Lord forever.
Write a short prayer of thanks for God's goodness in your life.

LESSON EIGHT

JESUS AS PROVIDER

MATTHEW 14:13-21

MATERIALS NEEDED

- Copy of *Spontaneous Melodrama* (pp. 70-71)
- Twinkies
- Bologna
- Wild and goofy costumes (optional)
- Flashlight
- Paper bags
- Take-home items (e.g. piece of bread, gummie fish, key chain)

Overview

This lesson is designed to teach students that Jesus loves them and desires to meet their needs.

Introduction (10-15 minutes)

This section introduces your students to the selected Scripture in a way that captures their interest and leads them into the study.

1) Select seven to ten student volunteers for the *Spontaneous Melodrama*, "Use my Twinkies" (pages 70-71).

Note: One of the great things about a melodrama is that it requires no preparation except for gathering a few props and costumes. This melodrama needs at least seven students and could use as many as thirty.

If you've never done a melodrama, you need to know the narrator plays a more important role than just reading the script. The narrator's use of timing, punctuation, emphasizing specific parts, interpreting the audience's reaction, and ad-lib instructions all help to make a humorous melodrama.

When you select volunteers for the speaking and acting parts, choose students who are uninhibited and willing to repeat silly lines and perform senseless tasks.

To prepare:

• Read through the script prior to your meeting time to give you an idea of what the characters do, and the students you might choose for the parts.

Feel free to adapt the script to best facilitate the students in your group, or to include specific "inside jokes" that your group may appreciate.

• After you've selected your characters, have them stand offstage until they are "read" onto the scene.

• Ask your audience to cheer for the actors. This will encourage the actors and will also get the audience more involved.

2) Perform the melodrama, using props and, if possible, costumes as suggested in the Materials Needed section for a stronger visual and humorous effect.

3) Before moving on, applaud and thank the stars of the melodrama. To make the transition to the next section, say, **Obviously this isn't exactly what happened, so open your Bibles to John chapter six and we'll read what really happened.**

4) Read John 6:1-15 aloud to your students.

Participation (10-15 minutes)
This section helps your students to experience the frustration of being unable to accomplish a goal because they don't have everything they need.

1) Divide the students into five groups. If your group is smaller than ten, divide students into pairs or stay in one group.

2) Darken the room, turning off all lights and pulling down all shades.

3) Give each group one paper bag that contains a different part of a flashlight:

• one bag contains the first battery
• one bag contains the second battery
• one bag contains the flashlight bulb
• one bag contains the flashlight casing
• one bag contains the flashlight top

4) Explain to your students that the main need for the moment is light. Turning on the room lights is not an option. Have them discuss in their groups the potential options for light.

5) After groups have discussed the options, direct them to pull the items out of their bags. Ask each group the following questions:

a) Can your group's item meet our need for light?

b) What can your item do by itself?

Observation (5-10 minutes)
This section reinforces the truth that even a small part (like a flashlight piece) is capable of great things when it's in the right hands.

1) With the room still dark, have one student from each group bring the group's item to you. It's best to do this one group at a time. Walk slowly around the room as you ask each group to bring its part to you. This will force the students to follow your voice in order to locate you.

2) Assemble the flashlight after you've gathered all five parts.

3) Turn the flashlight on and shine the beam around to identify each group.

Instruction (5-10 minutes)
This section helps your students understand that Jesus is the ultimate provider of our needs, that we don't need to look elsewhere to get our needs met, and that Jesus can use what we have to do great things.

1) While remaining in the dark, use the flashlight to read aloud Matthew 14:13-21, Matthew's account of the feeding of the five thousand.

2) Shine the flashlight on your face and say something such as this: **On that day, Jesus performed a miracle and provided for the needs of the crowd. Jesus still performs miracles and provides for your needs today.**

3) Then say, **Based on this story in God's Word, Jesus gives us two principles we can apply to our lives. They are simple to understand but tough to put into practice. Jesus' message includes these truths:**

a) "Don't worry, I'm right here with you."

b) "Give me what you have and I'll do something with it."

4) Have your students share any other thoughts they have about the story.

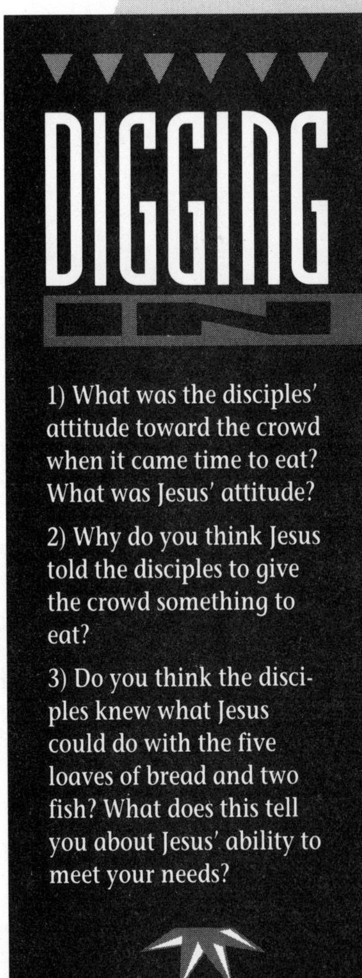

1) What was the disciples' attitude toward the crowd when it came time to eat? What was Jesus' attitude?

2) Why do you think Jesus told the disciples to give the crowd something to eat?

3) Do you think the disciples knew what Jesus could do with the five loaves of bread and two fish? What does this tell you about Jesus' ability to meet your needs?

Application (5 minutes)
This section provides your students with an opportunity to remember the message by giving them an object that will trigger the truth that Jesus provides for their needs.

Give each student an item to take home that will remind him or her of one of the two truths of Jesus' message, and triggers the big idea that Jesus provides for his and her needs. These items could be candy gummie fish, a piece of bread (dipped in resin so it won't grow moldy), a fish-shaped key chain, or other appropriate objects.

SPONTANEOUS MELODRAMA

Characters

Jesus
Simon
Judas
Timmy
Smiling Hill
Pin
Crowd (1-20 students*)
Disciples (1-10 students*)

*(*Depending on the number of students you have and the room you have for a stage.)*

Props

Paper bag
Costumes*
Twinkies
Bologna

**(Optional, but very effective. Be creative! The more ridiculous, the better.)*

Use My Twinkies

A Melodrama
Loosely based on John 6:1-15

(The Smiling Hill should already be onstage. Jesus and disciples enter as narrator begins reading. Jesus is carrying a paper bag.)

One day Jesus was hanging out with His disciples near Lake Galilee. Jesus was looking over the lake and whistling a pleasant tune. All of the disciples, except for Judas, were performing jumping jacks in an attempt to show who was the strongest and greatest disciple. Judas was counting out loud the number of jumping jacks the others were doing. Judas was always counting. He even could count in several different languages.

As Jesus was whistling and the disciples were doing jumping jacks and Judas was counting (*enter crowd*), a large crowd began to move toward Jesus. As the crowd got closer, the disciples stopped jumping and shouted, "Crowd, sit down."

Jesus frowned at the disciples and raised His eyebrows. The disciples knew what this meant so they shouted, "Crowd, *please* sit down." The crowd was thankful the disciples were polite and they shouted, "Thank you, disciples." The disciples shouted back, "You're welcome, crowd."

For the next ten seconds, the crowd and the disciples shouted greetings and exclamations back and forth. Judas counted the ten seconds out loud so all could hear. (*The crowd should now be sitting down.*)

After the pleasant exchange, Jesus sat on the Smiling Hill. The Hill smiled. The crowd shouted, "Nice smile." The disciples answered for the Hill and said, "Thank you, crowd." To Jesus' surprise, the Smiling Hill had the hiccups. It hiccuped with convulsions for fifteen seconds, but kept smiling the entire time. Jesus was still sitting on the Hill and was tossed back and forth.

After the Hill stopped hiccuping, Judas approached Jesus, put his foot on the Smiling Hill, and said, "There are at least five thousand people here, and they're all hungry."

Jesus put His right hand over His eyes to block the sun and scanned the crowd. He said, "Excellent counting, Judas." Judas smiled. He took his foot off the Smiling Hill and said, "Thank You, Jesus, that was so kind of You to notice my excellent counting." Judas put his other foot on the Smiling Hill.

Jesus said, "You're welcome." Both the crowd and the disciples gave Judas and Jesus high fives for being so polite to one another. After the clapping died down, Jesus said to Judas, "Is there a local 7-11 where you could buy

Slurpees and beef jerky for all these people?"

Judas said, "That's my favorite store. I love those numbers." The crowd groaned because that was such a dumb joke. Just then, the Smiling Hill sneezed and sprayed moisture over the crowd. The crowed groaned again. Judas said, "We would all have to work for 418 hours, 37 minutes, and 19 seconds at minimum wage to have enough money to buy all these people food." The crowd and disciples gave Judas high fives, not for his quick mathematical addition, but because he could remember such a long sentence for this melodrama.

Just then Simon, another one of Jesus' disciples, jumped to his feet and rushed over to Jesus. He put his foot on Smiling Hill, who was still smiling. Simon pointed to a boy in the crowd named Timmy and said, "There is a boy with four Twinkies and three pieces of bologna." (*Timmy should be sitting with the crowd, carrying the bologna and Twinkies.*)

Jesus said, "Stand up, boy." Timmy stood up and walked over to Jesus and put one foot on the Smiling Hill. When Timmy wasn't looking, Judas stole one piece of bologna and quickly shoved it into his mouth. Jesus held open a paper bag for Timmy to put his food in. As Timmy dropped his food into the bag, he noticed he was missing a piece of bologna. Timmy stood there looking confused for ten seconds. Judas counted off the seconds silently, but mouthed the numbers so Timmy knew when to stop looking confused.

Timmy then looked bewildered, perplexed, and mystified, which were really the same looks as confused because those words were in the thesaurus under the word "confused." Timmy now looked more confused, but the crowd understood and gave him some more high fives. Simon then shouted, "Judas stole the bologna. I saw him." The crowd quickly turned to look at Judas. The crowd said "Ooh" and "Aah." Just then, the Smiling Hill burped. This silenced the crowd. It was so quiet you could hear a pin drop. (*Enter Pin.*) Just then the Pin dropped to the floor making a loud noise. The crowd groaned because of the dumb gag. The Pin groaned because of its lousy part in the melodrama. Everyone was still looking at Judas. Judas looked frightened—so frightened that his knees were shaking. Jesus said, "Relax, man. This won't be the only time you'll be in trouble."

Jesus then said, "Everyone lay on your back." The crowd shouted in unison, "Only if You say please." Jesus smiled and winked at the Smiling Hill because He knew His good manners were rubbing off on the crowd. Jesus said, "Please!" And everyone laid down.

Jesus then said, "Put your right foot up, put your right foot down, put your left foot up and move it all around." The crowd followed Jesus' instructions. (*Jesus may need to repeat this.*) The crowd smiled because they knew that someday they would be mentioned as part of the first ever hokey-pokey dance.

Jesus then said, "Please! Everyone sit up." Jesus held the paper bag in front of the crowd and thanked God for the food, saying, "Thanks, God, for this food." The crowd cheered the prayer. Jesus began to hand out tons of bologna and Twinkies. (Imaginary of course—this is a skit, not the real thing.) Each person from the crowd gladly accepted the imaginary food and ate with imaginary delight.

After everyone had enough to eat, Jesus said to His disciples, "Gather the leftover bologna and Twinkies so nothing is wasted." The disciples skipped and whistled around the crowd, collecting the imaginary food. They gathered up enough imaginary food to fill twelve imaginary baskets.

When the crowd realized they had just witnessed a miracle, everyone looked bewildered, perplexed, and mystified. Timmy smiled because he recognized that look. The crowd shook the look off their faces and said, "Wow! Incredible! Never in my whole life!"

The crowd stood to their feet and cheered wildly. Jesus and His disciples left during the commotion. The crowd picked up the Smiling Hill and walked offstage. Timmy was left alone . . . still smiling. He said, "This must be the prophet who came to save us!"

The Smiling Hill shouted from a distance, "Thank you." The observing audience shouted, "You're welcome." And everyone gave the Pin high fives to close out the show. The end.

LESSON NINE

JESUS AS FORGIVER

JOHN 7:53—8:11

MATERIALS NEEDED

- Copies of *The World's Most Wanted* (pages 77-78)
- Five copies per student of *I Need Forgiveness* (page 79)
- Chalk and chalkboard or equivalent

Overview

This lesson is designed to help students understand that Jesus died for their sins, and that the power of forgiveness is liberating.

Introduction (5-10 minutes)

In this section your students will read about some infamous "bad guys," and then rank these people's crimes on the basis of which ones your students find the most despicable.

1) Hand each student a copy of *The World's Most Wanted* (pages 77-78).

2) Give students a few minutes to complete their handouts.

3) As students work, arrange for a few of them to make remarks such as "There's no one crime worse than another. They're all terrible." Acknowledge their accurate observations, but challenge them to complete their handouts. Encourage all of your students to look for specific examples of why some of these crimes may be worse than others.

4) Ask people to explain their choices. Your students will probably add their own comments about various crimes they've heard about; so be prepared for a brief tangent. Chances are that most of your students will see that all these crimes are equally horrible. Say something such as this: **All these crimes are evil, but some actions may seem unusually cruel to us.**

Participation (15-20 minutes)

This section will help students to see that while the consequences of sin are different, everyone is guilty of doing wrong.

1) As a group, choose one of the characters from *The World's Most Wanted* handout to put on trial.

2) Once that decision has been made, announce the need for a jury. Call different people to come to the front to participate in the jury selection process. The rest of the group will decide who will be members of the jury. Encourage students to keep track of the answers potential jury members give.

3) Ask your jury members to stand in a line, facing the rest of the group. To select the jury, go down the line and ask each person the following questions. Say something like this: **I'll ask each of you the same questions. Answer only yes or no. Don't give any explanations.**

4) Once students understand their roles, begin questioning the jury. You may use the following questions or make up similar ones to ask. Notice the progression in the questions. This is to make sure that each potential jury member is guilty of some wrongdoing. Add other questions if necessary.

- Have you ever murdered anyone?
- Have you ever gone on a shooting spree in order to get revenge?
- Have you ever robbed a bank?
- Have you ever embezzled money?
- Have you ever snitched a piece of candy from the bulk food bins at the grocery store?
- Have you ever received a speeding ticket?
- Have you ever jaywalked?
- Have you ever "forgotten" a few details when telling your parents about the party you went to?
- Have you ever talked back to your parents?

5) When each person has finally admitted being guilty of one of these crimes, tell the rest of the group that it's time to select the best possible jury. You want jury members who are perfect, who haven't done anything wrong. Give the group a minute or two to reach a decision. The group may or may not disqualify everyone from the jury. If not, encourage students to explain why they think someone isn't guilty of doing wrong.

6) Regardless of the outcome, announce that you're declaring a mistrial because none of these people is perfect. Each one is guilty of doing something wrong. And since you were looking for the perfect jury, no one qualifies.

7) To move into the next section, say something such as this: **When it comes to God's standards, none of us qualifies there either.**

Instruction (10 minutes)

This section helps your students to understand that our sin makes us guilty before God. Jesus is the one who forgives our sin and acts in our defense before God.

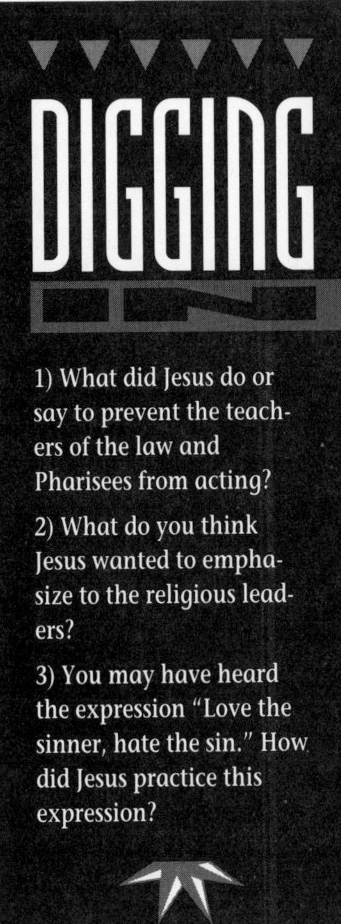

1) What did Jesus do or say to prevent the teachers of the law and Pharisees from acting?

2) What do you think Jesus wanted to emphasize to the religious leaders?

3) You may have heard the expression "Love the sinner, hate the sin." How did Jesus practice this expression?

1) Begin by saying, **The Bible says that we're all guilty of sin** (read Romans 3:23 to the group). **But there's good news: Jesus comes to our defense. Without Him we all are as guilty as the people who have committed the worst crimes. If it wasn't for Jesus, we would have no hope for forgiveness.**

2) Read aloud John 8:1-11.

3) Make sure the students understand Jesus' forgiveness of this woman.

4) Get some feedback from the students. They may or may not see a big difference between forgiving someone for adultery and forgiving someone for one of the crimes on the handout, *The World's Most Wanted.*

5) Continue the discussion by asking one or more of the following questions:

> a) Although Jesus forgives all sins, are there some sins that carry more severe consequences than others? Give an example.
>
> b) How do we ask for forgiveness? After getting some answers, read the following passage:

If we confess our sins, he is faithful and just and will forgive us our sins and purify us from all unrighteousness (I John 1:9).

> c) Based on I John 1:9, what is the purpose of confessing our sins?

6) Refer to the following Scripture and point out the good news that God not only forgives our sins, but also forgets our sins:

I, even I, am he who blots out your transgressions, for my own sake, and remembers your sins no more (Isaiah 43:25).

Observation (5-10 minutes)

This section helps your students to see, hear, and understand that God not only forgives, He forgets.

1) Have your students, one by one, draw a symbol that represents their "crimes" on the chalkboard, under the heading "Forgive me for . . ." Appoint another student to be "God." As each "criminal" asks for forgiveness, "God" walks over to the chalkboard and erases his or her crime off the chalkboard, illustrating the forgetfulness aspect of forgiveness. Then

"God" turns to the repentant sinner and says, "Forgive you for what?"

2) Point out to your students that no matter how many times they come up to the chalkboard and inscribe their crimes, God can erase the sin. Even sins we struggle with over and over again are forgiven by God as we come to Him for His mercy.

Application (5 minutes)

This section provides your students with some reminders of the power of God's forgiveness and gives them a tool they can use to further understand Jesus' forgiveness.

1) Give each student five copies of the handout *I Need Forgiveness* (page 79).

2) Have them complete the first copy now.

3) Encourage students to complete the other copies each night before they go to bed.

After reading the following five descriptions, rank the men according to who appears to be the worst criminal. Give the worst person a one, the second worst two, and so on.

_____Al "Scarface" Capone

_____The Boston Strangler

_____Billy the Kid

_____Charles Manson

_____Son of Sam

Al "Scarface" Capone *(1899–1947)*

Al Capone was one of the most brutal gangsters of his day. He bragged that he "owned" the Chicago police during the Prohibition years. It has been estimated that over half the city police were on his payroll. At one time, Capone single-handedly beat up the mayor of Chicago on the steps of city hall, and the nearby police officers turned their backs. During his mob reign, it has been estimated that he ordered the death of more than five hundred men, and over one thousand people died in his bootleg alcohol wars.

Albert Desalvo, *The Boston Strangler (1933–1973)*

Within two years, Albert Desalvo killed thirteen women in Boston, Massachusetts. He used a variety of methods to talk his way into homes of women who were living alone. One time, for example, he pretended to be a police officer to get into a woman's home. Once inside, he then sexually assaulted and strangled the victim. Women in Boston grew so afraid that they refused to open their doors. He was eventually caught, sent to prison for life, and stabbed to death in his cell.

William "Billy the Kid" Bonney *(1859–1881)*

Although he has been portrayed as a good guy, Bonney was a fierce killer. Billy the Kid's real name was Henry McCarty. He took on the alias of William Bonney after he shot a man to death in a quarrel. On the run, Billy the Kid was hired by a rancher who became his friend. When the rancher was killed in a frontier feud, Bill swore he would "get" everyone that had anything to do with this man's death. After Billy the Kid's spree of revenge, he ended up killing a lawman. He was caught for this murder and eventually jailed. As he waited in jail for his hanging, he escaped and killed two deputies.

Charles Manson *(1934–)*

Followers of cult leader Charles Manson entered a Los Angeles, California, estate and murdered five people, including a pregnant woman. These five were shot, stabbed, and clubbed to death. The killers used the victims' blood to write crazy words on the walls. During the slaughter, one of the killers kept screaming, "I am the devil and I came to do the devil's work!" Two nights later, this incredible scene was repeated at another home. The murders were eventually traced back to the Manson "family." His cultlike group experimented with drugs and conducted bizarre religious ceremonies built around Charles Manson as a Christlike figure. He and some of his followers are in prison today.

Son of Sam *(1953–)*

This man terrorized the city of New York. He fired a total of thirty-one bullets into thirteen young women and men, killing six and severely wounding seven in eight separate attacks. Generally the victims were young girls or couples parked in cars at night. After he was caught, he pleaded guilty and was sentenced to life in prison.

I NEED FORGIVENESS

If we confess our sins, he . . . will forgive us our sins. I John 1:9a

1) Tell God: "I need forgiveness. I confess to you the following sins:

____

____

____

____

____ Please forgive me!"

. . . He is faithful and just and will . . . purify us from all unrighteousness.
(I John 1:9b)

2) Take a minute to thank God for forgiving you and cleansing you from the wrongs you have done.

I, even I, am he who blots out your transgressions, for my own sake,
and remembers your sins no more.
(Isaiah 43:25)

3) Since God forgets your sins, throw this sheet away so that you'll never see these confessed sins again.

I NEED FORGIVENESS

If we confess our sins, he . . . will forgive us our sins. I John 1:9a

1) Tell God: "I need forgiveness. I confess to you the following sins:

____

____

____

____

____ Please forgive me!"

. . . He is faithful and just and will . . . purify us from all unrighteousness.
(I John 1:9b)

2) Take a minute to thank God for forgiving you and cleansing you from the wrongs you have done.

I, even I, am he who blots out your transgressions, for my own sake,
and remembers your sins no more.
(Isaiah 43:25)

3) Since God forgets your sins, throw this sheet away so that you'll never see these confessed sins again.

LESSON TEN

JESUS AS HERO

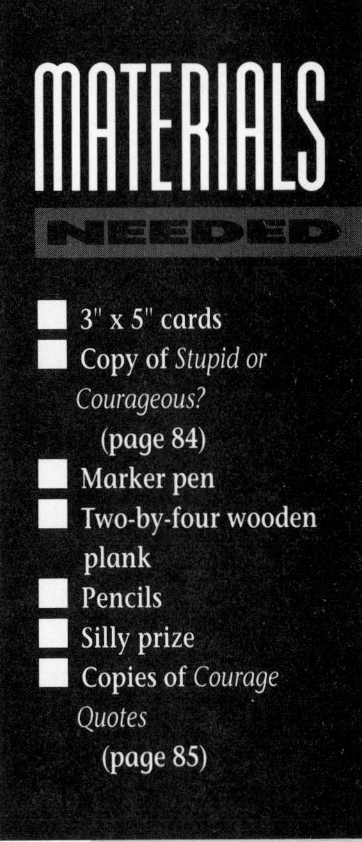

MATERIALS NEEDED

- 3" x 5" cards
- Copy of *Stupid or Courageous?* (page 84)
- Marker pen
- Two-by-four wooden plank
- Pencils
- Silly prize
- Copies of *Courage Quotes* (page 85)

Overview

This lesson is designed to get students talking about fear. It will also help them to understand that Jesus wasn't afraid because He was confident of God's plan. It also challenges students to replace their fears with trust and confidence in God's plan for their lives.

Introduction (5-10 minutes)
This section gets your students thinking about the differences between courage and stupidity.

1) Break your students into four groups.

2) Have four 3" x 5" cards ready for each group (sixteen cards total). For each four-card set, write the word "stupid" on two of the cards, and the word "courageous" on the other two cards.

3) Select two student volunteers from each team. Each of these students is given a "stupid" card and a "courageous" card. Position the two students from the same team so that they can't see each other's responses.

4) Explain to the students that you will be reading a list of actions that can be described by either of these words (see *Stupid or Courageous*? page 84). As you read the list, the student volunteers must decide which of the actions are stupid and which are acts of courage.

5) The student volunteers immediately vote on each action by holding up either the "stupid" or "courageous" card.

6) Award 100 points to each team every time its two volunteers agree in their answers. Likewise, deduct 100 points every time the teammates disagree. It's possible for a team to end up with a negative score.

7) If you want, add some of your own actions to the list that relate specifically to your area, your students' schools, or your church.

Participation (10-15 minutes)
This section involves your students in an activity that plays upon the emotions of fear and trust.

1) Tell your students that it's time for a skydiving lesson. Select three student volunteers and send them out of the room. Encourage the other students to cheer wildly. (This will have a great effect on the students participating in the game.)

2) One at a time, bring each volunteer back into the room and ask him or her to stand on a sturdy two-by-four wooden plank that is lifted up by two strong guys. The person standing on the board should use a leader's shoulders as a brace so he or she won't fall. The board is lifted up about three feet, and then the contestant is asked to jump into a small circle for five points. The board is lifted higher and the contestant jumps again for 10 points.

The last time, for 100 points, he or she must jump blindfolded. The strong guys, however, only lift the board two or three inches off the ground, while stooping down really low, which gives the blindfolded volunteer the feeling that he or she is several feet off the ground. Most students that jump will usually scream or yell because they believe they are going to fall a considerable distance to the floor.

3) Interview the participating students and have them share their feelings about the experience.

Observation (5-10 minutes)
This section helps your students to understand the things that they fear and identify reasons for their fears.

1) Ask for three volunteers to come to the front for a "screen test" for expressions of fears. Instruct your volunteers to turn their backs to the group and come up with their expressions. Then at your signal, they're to turn around and show their fearful expressions. If you'd like, have these volunteers express mild surprise, fear, and sheer terror. Have the group vote for the best screen test, and award a silly prize to the winner.

2) Have students discuss the things that they fear. List these things on a chalkboard as they share.

3) As an option, you might want to bring in a white mouse or even a snake for students to handle, or not handle, depending on how much they're afraid of mice or snakes. Get kids to talk about their fears.

4) As you move into the next section, say something such as this: **Sometimes if we can identify the source of a fear, it becomes easier to face. And as Christians, we have the best resource for facing our fears.**

Instruction (5-10 minutes)

This section gets your students to see Jesus' courage as He had faith in God's plan for Him.

1) Read aloud Mark 14:43-51. If possible, encourage (don't force) someone in the group who is normally shy or quiet to read the selected passage. If the person doesn't feel coerced, this might be a great exercise in courage for him or her.

2) Point out some key facts of this passage by saying, **Jesus knew this was going to happen. Jesus could have easily run or slipped away from the guards before they got Him. Look at the disciples—the Bible says they were so scared, they ran away.**

3) Emphasize the big idea that's printed on the bottom of page 85: Let your FEARS be replaced by confidence in God's plan for your life. **Seeing the courage of Jesus in this situation illustrates His confidence in God's plan for His life. His fear was replaced with confidence in God. And we can do the same thing too.**

4) Have your students share other thoughts they might have about the story.

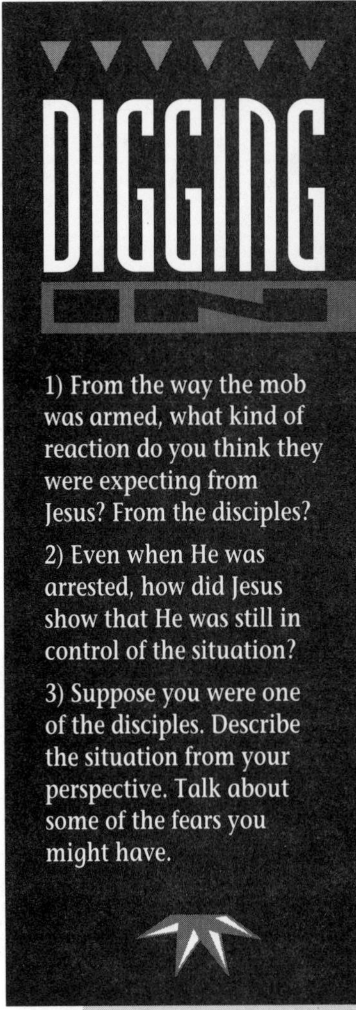

DIGGING
IN
1) From the way the mob was armed, what kind of reaction do you think they were expecting from Jesus? From the disciples?
2) Even when He was arrested, how did Jesus show that He was still in control of the situation?
3) Suppose you were one of the disciples. Describe the situation from your perspective. Talk about some of the fears you might have.

Application (5-10 minutes)

This section gets your students to personalize courage by writing a definition of courage.

1) Have students read aloud some of their favorite quotes from *Courage Quotes* (see page 85).

2) After the reading of the quotes, have the students circle the quotes they identify with the most.

3) Next, have your students write their own definitions of courage.

4) Collect their definitions, so you can compile their courage definitions and pass out copies at your next meeting. Check also with your pastor to see if you can publish a few of the students' definitions in the church bulletin the following week.

Stupid or courageous?

Bungee jumping

Sticking your hand in a blender

Strapping a prime rib to your back and running through a lion's cage

Eating a raw onion

Breaking up over the phone

Breaking up in person

Bringing your Bible to school

Standing up for your beliefs

Going on a blind date

Being a friend to someone who may not be too popular

Showing up for football practice without a helmet

Telling your mom that her cooking stinks

Cheering for the opposite team at a football game

Flying a jet with the Blue Angels

Taking a dare to ______________ (fill in the blank yourself)

Holding a rattlesnake

Kissing your Aunt Fi Fi on the lips

Walking on hot coals

Eating a bean burrito on your first date

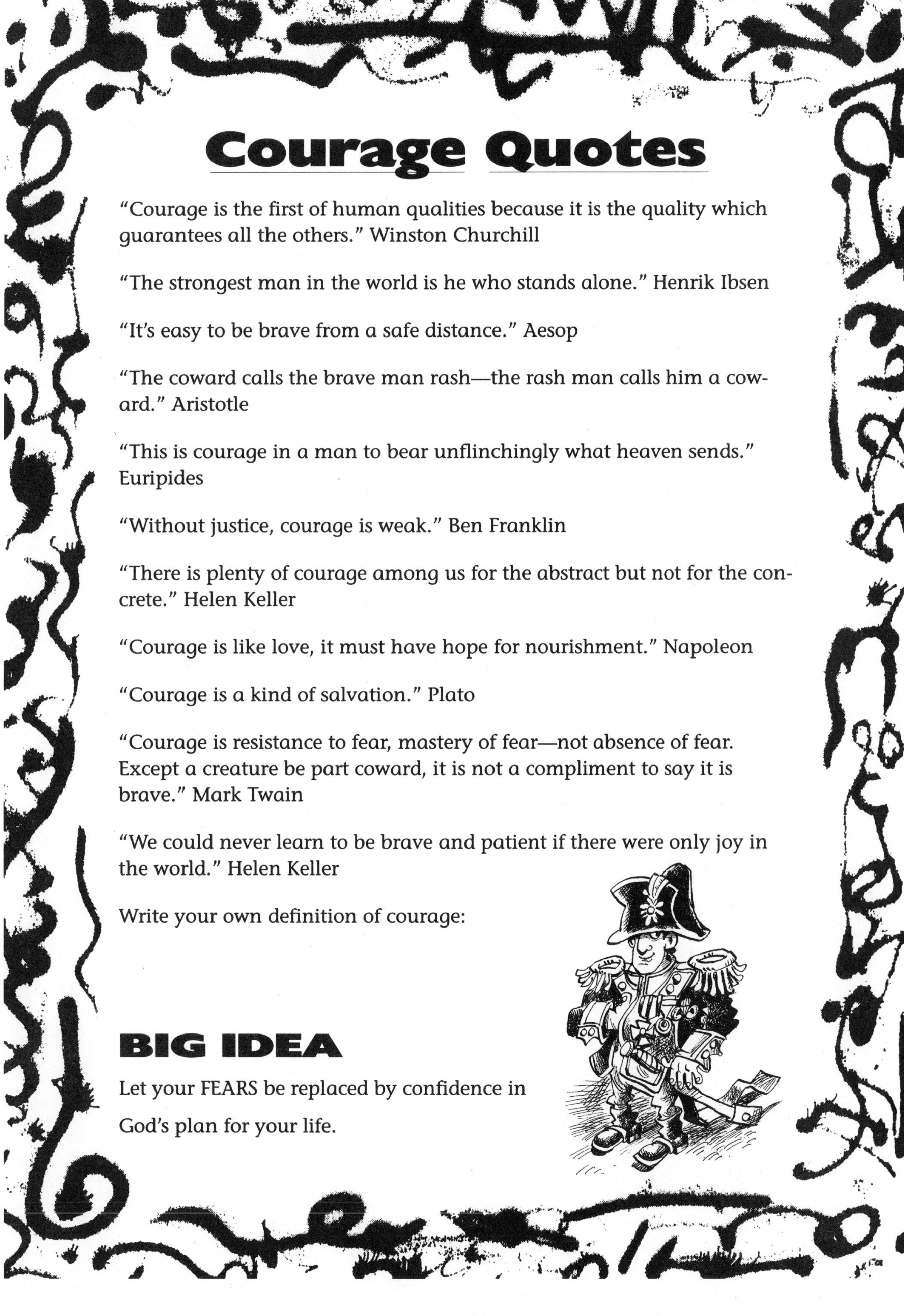

Courage Quotes

"Courage is the first of human qualities because it is the quality which guarantees all the others." Winston Churchill

"The strongest man in the world is he who stands alone." Henrik Ibsen

"It's easy to be brave from a safe distance." Aesop

"The coward calls the brave man rash—the rash man calls him a coward." Aristotle

"This is courage in a man to bear unflinchingly what heaven sends." Euripides

"Without justice, courage is weak." Ben Franklin

"There is plenty of courage among us for the abstract but not for the concrete." Helen Keller

"Courage is like love, it must have hope for nourishment." Napoleon

"Courage is a kind of salvation." Plato

"Courage is resistance to fear, mastery of fear—not absence of fear. Except a creature be part coward, it is not a compliment to say it is brave." Mark Twain

"We could never learn to be brave and patient if there were only joy in the world." Helen Keller

Write your own definition of courage:

BIG IDEA

Let your FEARS be replaced by confidence in God's plan for your life.

LESSON ELEVEN

JESUS AS SAVIOR

JOHN 19:1-30

MATERIALS NEEDED

- Five sheets of poster board
- Rope, twine, or string
- 8-foot roll or sheet of red paper
- Marker
- Chalk
- Tomato paste
- Canned spinach
- Clam chowder
- Canned cream corn
- Mustard
- Drop cloth
- Cellophane tape

Overview

This lesson is designed to show students that their sin keeps them from God. It also helps them see that Jesus died for their sins so they can have a relationship with God.

Introduction (10 minutes)

This section hooks your students' attention toward the topic of sin.

1) In large letters, write five different sins on the five pieces of poster board—one sin per piece. Here are some examples:

Lying
Cheating
Stealing
Pride
Premarital sex

2) Tape each of the five sheets horizontally on a wall so students can see them.

3) Have your students arrange the five sins in a vertical column as they rank the sins on a scale of 1 to 5 (with 5 being the worst sin). The sin that's ranked a 5 should be at the bottom of the column. Encourage students to move around the sheets of paper as they decide on the different ranks. Since a unanimous ranking is rare, be prepared to be democratic.

4) Be ready for a few of your students to remind you that, in the eyes of God,

sin is sin and there's no one sin worse than another. If this happens, encourage students to rank the sins according to potential consequences the sin has toward themselves and others, or how seriously society condemns them.

5) After your students have ranked the sins, remove the sheets of poster board from the wall.

Participation (20 minutes)
This section teaches your students that there is no winner with sin. It's not a game, and it does have consequences.

1) Place all five sheets of poster board on the floor as shown in the illustration on page 91.

2) These "sin signs" will serve as a pseudo board game. Each sin represents a space on the game board.

3) Directly in front of the sin signs, place two pieces of rope, twine, or string about twelve inches apart (see the "Floor Layout" diagram on page 91).

4) Place a piece of paper with the word "sinful" on it by one piece of rope and another piece of paper with the word "sinless" by the other piece of rope.

5) Next, line up the players in front of the "sinless" rope. (Note: If you have a large group, divide into four teams, and have one person from each team stand by each sin. That way, you will be able to use five students from each team, or twenty students in all.)

6) To start the game, one player from each team must jump from the "sinless" rope to the "sinful" rope and shout out, "I can make myself like God." This statement is based on the serpent's lies to Eve in Genesis 3:5.

7) Once they've made the jump, the serious game playing begins. Explain to the students they will be given points based on the first player or team to complete the consequences of every sin. In other words, if there are four teams, four players from each team will be racing to be the first to complete the sin's consequence and move on to the next square. Assign a scorekeeper for each team.

8) Assign "consequences" that need to be performed for each sin. Use the suggested activities listed here, or adjust them to your group.

Sin	*Consequence*
Lying	Spin around five times
Cheating	Do three push-ups
Stealing	Perform ten jumping jacks

Pride	Hop around for ten seconds
Premarital sex	Run around screaming "Ouch"

9) Directly after the last sin square, place two pieces of rope at least six feet apart. Write the words "sinful" and "forgiven" on two separate sheets of paper and place one sheet at each rope (similar to what you did in steps three and four).

10) Explain that the winner of the game—no matter what the score is—will be the person or team that can jump from the "sinful" rope to the "forgiven" rope. The jump must be a standing jump rather than a running jump. Make sure the distance between the two ropes would be impossible for any student to jump across, no matter how athletic he or she is.

11) After each group has made unsuccessful attempts to jump across the ropes, have the students sit down. Don't declare a winner. Keep the game set up for the Application section.

Observation (5-10 minutes)

This section helps your students to see the mess created by wickedness and sin.

1) Before beginning this section,

a) position a chalkboard (preferably a whiteboard) near the two ropes around which the students are seated;

b) place a drop cloth underneath the chalkboard to catch the mess you will make.

2) Inform the students that the chalkboard represents the wonder of their lives—that they have been created in the likeness of God.

3) Explain that along with being created in God's image, each person also has to face up to the fact that he or she has sinned. Everyone is sinful by nature.

4) As you talk, splatter different types of food or color onto your chalkboard to graphically illustrate the mess of sin. For example, you could use these foods to illustrate the following sins:

- Tomato paste to illustrate lying
- Canned spinach to illustrate cheating
- Mustard to illustrate stealing
- Canned cream corn to illustrate pride
- Clam chowder to illustrate premarital sex

5) Emphasize that the disgusting mess they see illustrates how bad sin

looks in our lives.

6) Just a reminder to clean up the mess to keep the custodian from quitting!

Instruction (5-10 minutes)
This section helps your students to understand that Jesus provided for their need of a Savior by dying for their "mess," that is, their sins.

1) Read aloud John 19:1-30.

2) Tell your students, **Jesus' death on the cross finished the work He was sent to do. His death paid for our sins.**

3) Then say, **Jesus came to earth, lived, and died to provide you with a way to God. It's impossible to get to God without the Savior.**

4) Have your students share any other thoughts they have had during the story.

Application (5 minutes)
This section helps your students to see that the only way they can be saved from the eternal consequences of their wickedness is through the death of Christ.

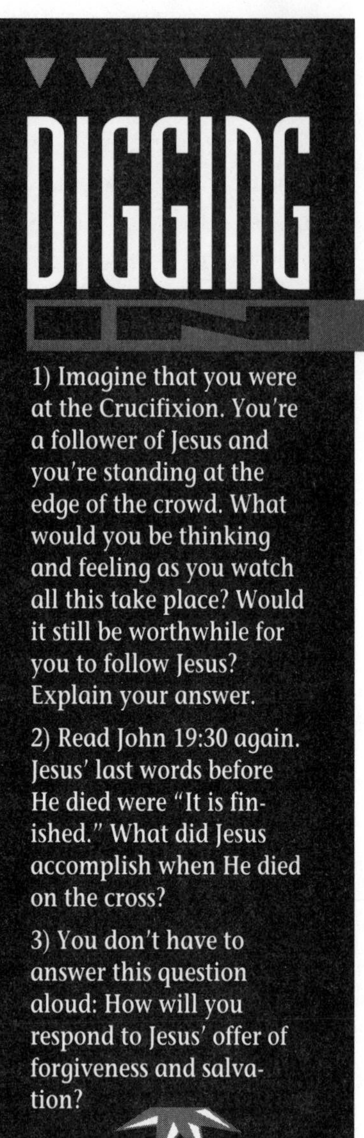

1) Imagine that you were at the Crucifixion. You're a follower of Jesus and you're standing at the edge of the crowd. What would you be thinking and feeling as you watch all this take place? Would it still be worthwhile for you to follow Jesus? Explain your answer.

2) Read John 19:30 again. Jesus' last words before He died were "It is finished." What did Jesus accomplish when He died on the cross?

3) You don't have to answer this question aloud: How will you respond to Jesus' offer of forgiveness and salvation?

1) Spread out your roll of red paper, or tape together eight sheets of red construction paper, and write some key salvation verses on the pieces of paper (for example, John 3:16; Romans 10:9; I John 1:9). The visual image of the red paper represents Christ's sacrifice that allows us access to God.

2) Place your paper between the two ropes, so it reaches across the ropes.

3) Have your students write their names on the strip of paper, indicating their need for Jesus' sacrifice and their commitment to Him.

4) Hang this paper in your youth room as a reminder of what is needed to have a right relationship with God.

Floor Layout

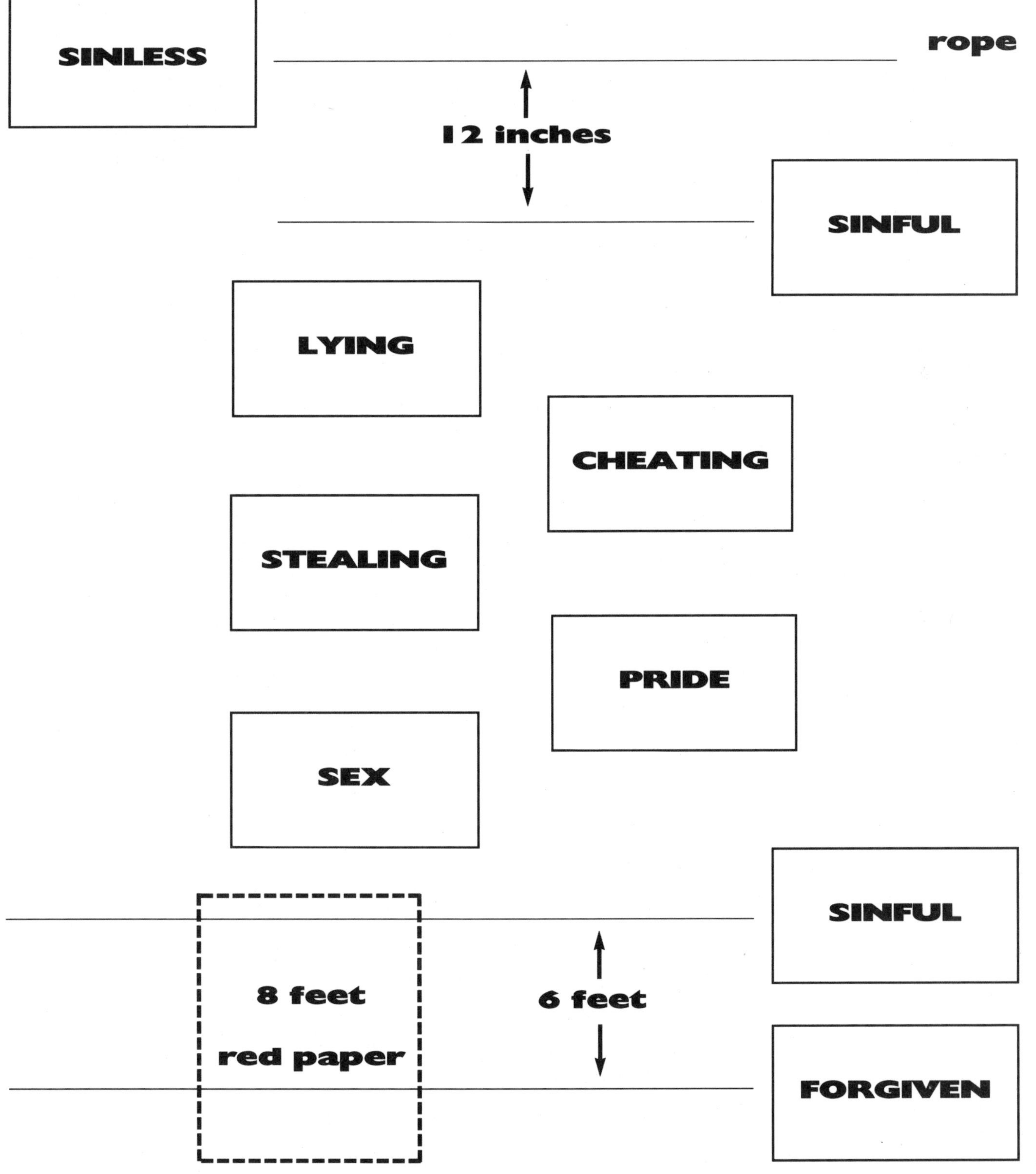

LESSON TWELVE

JESUS AS VICTOR

JOHN 20:1-29

MATERIALS NEEDED

- Humorous awards such as used trophies
- Supplies for selected game (see *Introduction*)
- Copy of the video *Rocky IV*
- TV
- VCR
- Copies of *Victory Work Sheet* (page 96)
- *Dear Jesus* letters from Lesson 1
- Candy for "contest" winner (optional)

Overview

This lesson is designed to show students that Jesus was victorious over death. Because of His victory, they too can be victorious and live eternally.

Introduction (10 minutes)
This section gets your students thinking about the terminology and concept of winning and being victorious.

1) Use either of the two following game ideas or come up with a game of your own. The emphasis isn't on the game itself, but on the outcome.

a) Create your own awards show. Your awards can be anything from candy to trophies. (You can purchase old, inexpensive trophies at local thrift stores; they serve as perfect humorous awards.) Give awards for categories such as the person who

- is most likely to shave off his or her dog's fur
- is most likely to shave his or her grandma's moustache
- is best at exaggerating stories
- is best excuse-maker for missing youth group
- has best laugh

b) Divide your students into two or more groups to compete in one or more of the following simple games:

- Darts
- Nerf basketball

- Eating contests (for example, banana, marshmallow, drinking a liter bottle of pop through a straw)
- Answering trivia questions
- Pictionary

2) Make a big deal about "winning" the awards or being victorious in the exciting Nerf basketball game. Interview students to find out how they felt about winning or losing. Ask, **Why do you think everyone likes to win?**

Observation (5-10 minutes)

This section gives your students a visual connection of the concept of being victorious.

1) Rent the movie *Rocky IV* from a local video store.

2) Show the scene at the end of the movie where Rocky is fighting the Russian boxer for the championship of the world. The fight goes back and forth between Rocky Balboa and the Russian, ending in a climactic scene with Rocky's victory. (Even though many of your students may have seen this movie, it's a perfect example of being victorious.)

3) If you are unable to get the video, here's an option. Select a volunteer and have him or her leave the room. Tell the rest of the class that the volunteer has been declared the winner of the pastor look-alike contest and deserves to be recognized for this great honor. Bring the volunteer back into the room to enormous cheers, and present him or her with a candy bar as the contest prize.

Participation (10-15 minutes)

This exercise gets all of your students actively involved in the Scriptures by acting out specific passages.

1) Say, **Now that we've seen a person experience victory, we're going to take a look at someone who experienced the greatest victory of all. This person is someone who is important to our lives.**

2) Break your students into four equal groups.

3) Assign each group one of the following passages:

a) John 20:1-9
b) John 20:10-18
c) John 20:19-23
d) John 20:24-29

4) Give each group adequate time to create a simple skit portraying what they have read and interpreted in the passage.

5) Allow each group to present its interpretation of the Resurrection story. Encourage the other groups to be supportive and cheer enthusiastically for each performance.

Instruction (5-10 minutes)
This section helps your students to understand that Jesus is victorious over sin and death because of the Resurrection. And because of the Resurrection, their faith has significance now and eternally.

Say, **Jesus' resurrection from the dead is one of the most important truths of Christianity. His resurrection means that He conquered and defeated death. In I Corinthians 15:54 it says, "Death has been swallowed up in victory." Jesus' resurrection also has other important meanings for your life. They are the following:**

> **a) Jesus kept His promises. He said He would die and rise again, and He did. Throughout the Bible, God and Jesus have been faithful to their promises.**
>
> **b) Your faith is worth something because of the Resurrection. The Bible says, "And if Christ has not been raised, our preaching is useless and so is your faith" (I Corinthians 15:14).**
>
> **c) You can be victorious over death by having eternal life. The Bible says, "For God so loved the world that he gave his one and only Son, that whoever believes in him shall not perish but have eternal life" (John 3:16).**

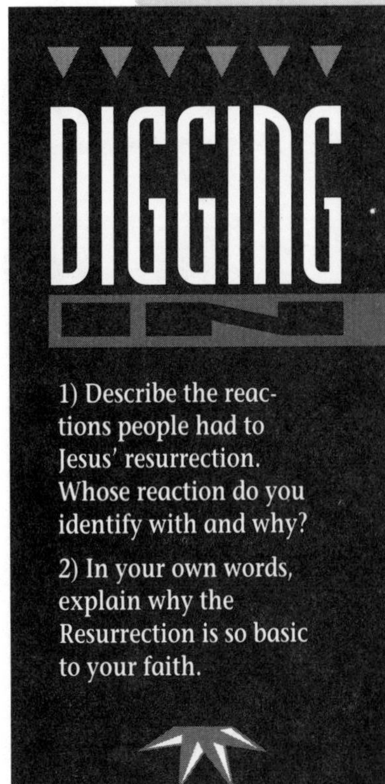

DIGGING
IN
1) Describe the reactions people had to Jesus' resurrection. Whose reaction do you identify with and why?
2) In your own words, explain why the Resurrection is so basic to your faith.

Application (5-10 minutes)
This section helps the students understand the personal appearances of Jesus after His resurrection and gives them an opportunity to consider what Jesus means to them personally, and how He can work in their lives.

1) Give each student a copy of the *Victory Work Sheet* (page 96).

2) Have them answer the questions.

3) Give them an opportunity to share some of their responses.

4) If you have enough time, bring closure to this series by having the students share what they've learned about Jesus over the last several weeks. Also, give back the letters the students wrote at the end of Lesson One, and have them share if their feelings about Jesus are any different now than they were when they first wrote the *Dear Jesus* letters.

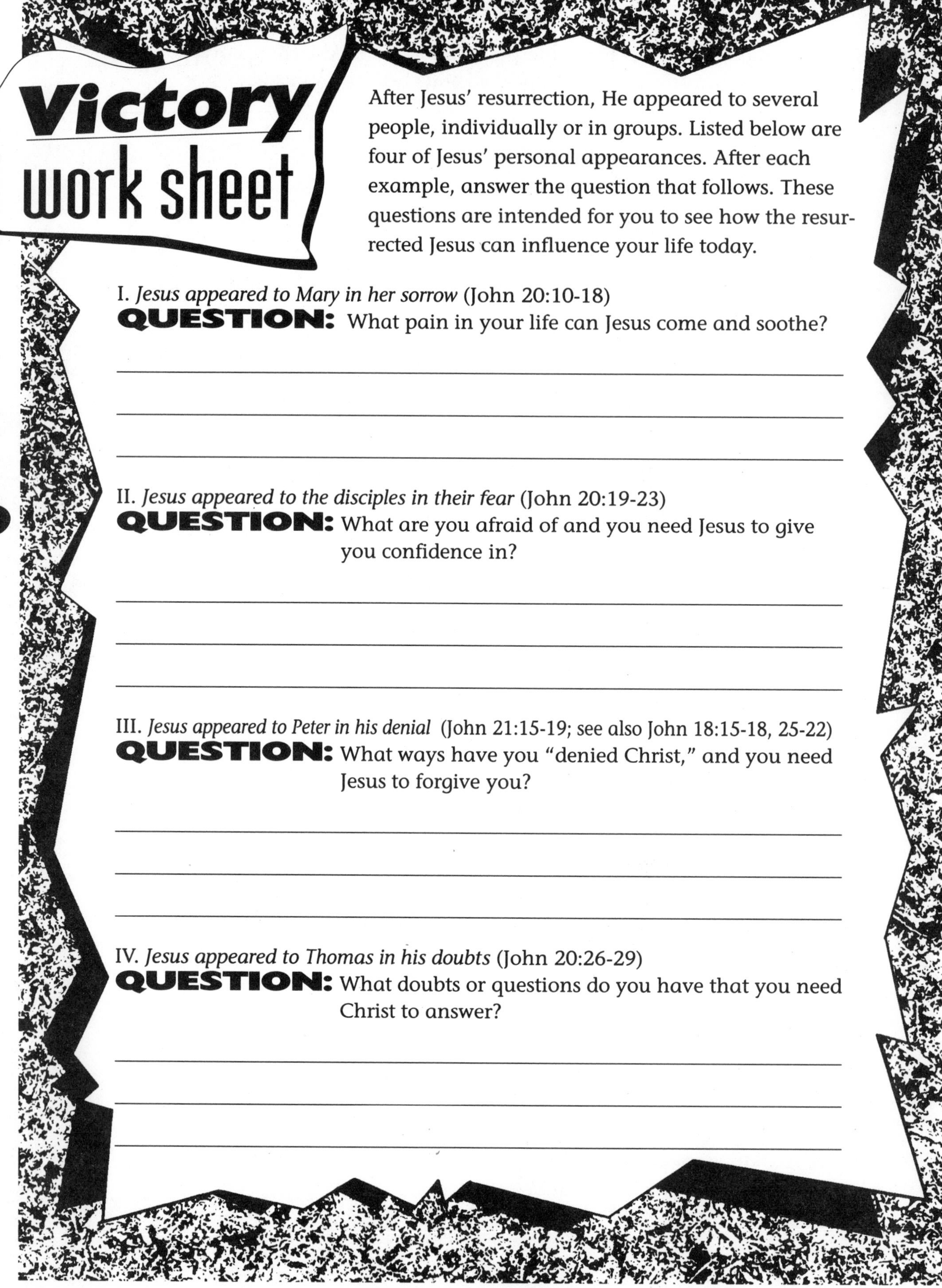

Victory work sheet

After Jesus' resurrection, He appeared to several people, individually or in groups. Listed below are four of Jesus' personal appearances. After each example, answer the question that follows. These questions are intended for you to see how the resurrected Jesus can influence your life today.

I. *Jesus appeared to Mary in her sorrow* (John 20:10-18)
QUESTION: What pain in your life can Jesus come and soothe?

____

____

____

II. *Jesus appeared to the disciples in their fear* (John 20:19-23)
QUESTION: What are you afraid of and you need Jesus to give you confidence in?

____

____

____

III. *Jesus appeared to Peter in his denial* (John 21:15-19; see also John 18:15-18, 25-22)
QUESTION: What ways have you "denied Christ," and you need Jesus to forgive you?

____

____

____

IV. *Jesus appeared to Thomas in his doubts* (John 20:26-29)
QUESTION: What doubts or questions do you have that you need Christ to answer?

____

____

____